Thank you for picking up my book. Your support means a lot, and I hope you find the read both enjoyable and insightful. Beyond being an author, my work extends into research and consultancy within organizational behavior and leadership. I engage with a broad spectrum of clients, from individuals to larger teams and organizations, offering guidance in leadership development.

For a deeper dive into my professional background and consulting philosophy, several websites are available. There, you'll also find my contact details. I'm eager to hear your thoughts on the book or discuss potential collaboration in leadership coaching.

Discover more about my work and other publications related to leadership and organizational behavior at my personal website, https://thomaspatrickhuber.com.

Learn about my specific approach to leadership coaching and consulting at https://elevateus.ch, the official website of my company.

Lastly, in case you want to reach out to me directly please send me an email at thomaspatrick@mac.com.

I appreciate your support in purchasing this book and look forward to connecting with you.

Wishing you an enlightening journey,

Thomas P Huber, PhD, MS ECS

Dedication

This book is dedicated to each and every one of us, forever students in the realm of leadership. While leadership may be mastered, it is never perfected. As global citizens working on changing the world and sustaining transformation, we all share a common commitment to learning, growing, and making our world a better place.

May the insights within these pages continue to nourish our hunger for knowledge and guide us on our ever-evolving path of leadership. Together, we embrace the journey of change and transformation, united by our dedication to becoming better leaders and making a positive impact on the world.

Foreword

I have had the privilege to learn about change management early in my career during my master's program. I fell in love with the notion that the only constant is change. I deeply believe in that saying and have experienced this in my life. While most of us, at some point, hope for a consistent, similar pattern or a constant state of affairs, reality is much more complicated and nuanced. Even in the smallest circumstances, life is constantly evolving and changing. It is life itself that is never the same from moment to moment.

So, what should we do about it? Well, we can meet this change head-on. We can learn to work with change, adapt to its ebbs and flows, and ultimately, we can embrace change. In fact, we can do more than embrace it; we can lead change – for ourselves and for others.

We can hope to manage change and navigate its challenges, but the true power lies in our ability to lead it. This book you hold in your hands is a testament to the belief that change is not something to be feared or resisted; rather, it is a force that can be harnessed and directed towards greater success and fulfillment.

In the following pages, you will embark on a journey that explores the art and science of leading change. Drawing from the experiences of change leaders and pioneers, as well as the latest insights from the field of change management, this book will equip you with the knowledge, tools, and strategies to navigate the ever-shifting landscape of change with confidence and competence.

As you delve into the chapters that follow, remember that change is not just an external force; it is an intrinsic part of our lives. By mastering the principles of change leadership, you empower yourself to not only adapt to change but also to shape it, to drive transformation, and to leave a lasting impact.

So, let us embrace the constant ebb and flow of life's changes, for it is through change that we find growth, innovation, and the opportunity to make our world a better place. May this book be your trusted companion on your journey to leading the change revolution, and may it inspire you to embrace change as a powerful force for good.

With anticipation and enthusiasm,

Thomas P Huber PhD MS ECS

Introduction

In modern business, change is not an anomaly; it is the bedrock upon which the ever-evolving landscape rests. The first step in our journey through "Leading the Change Revolution: Initiating and Sustaining Transformation" begins with a fundamental acknowledgment: change is an unceasing element, integral to the fabric of organizational life. Historically, change was often viewed as a series of isolated events, disruptions to be managed or challenges to be overcome. Today, however, this perception has shifted dramatically. In an era marked by rapid technological advancements, globalization, and evolving societal values, change has become a continuous force, driving progress and innovation at an unprecedented pace.

This constant state of flux presents a unique set of opportunities and challenges for organizations. The ability to anticipate, adapt to, and capitalize on change is no longer a luxury; it has become a necessity for survival and success. Those who view change as a sporadic disturbance are likely to find themselves unprepared and vulnerable in a world that demands agility and resilience. To thrive in this dynamic environment, organizations must foster a culture that does not merely tolerate change but actively embraces it. This involves a shift in mindset at every level, from the C-suite to the front lines. It requires a departure from traditional, linear thinking and a move towards a more flexible, adaptive approach.

Embracing change as a constant means recognizing that the business landscape of today is not the landscape of tomorrow. It requires a commitment to continuous learning, innovation, and evolution. It calls for leaders who are visionary yet pragmatic, capable of navigating their organizations through uncharted territories with confidence and foresight. We will explore the various dimensions of change as a constant force. We will examine how this perspective reshapes strategies, decision-making processes, and leadership styles. We will also consider the tools and frameworks that can help organizations and leaders to not just survive but thrive in a world where change is the only constant. Embracing change as a constant is the first step in mastering the art of change leadership. It is the foundation upon which successful, adaptive, and resilient organizations are built. As we embark on this journey together, let us embrace this paradigm shift with an open mind and a willingness to transform, not just our organizations but ourselves as leaders in this dynamic, ever-changing world.

As we move forward from understanding change as a constant, the next critical element in our journey is recognizing the transformative power of effective change leadership. This power is not just about managing or coping with change; it's about harnessing it, guiding it, and using it to propel an organization forward. In this era of relentless transformation, the role of a change leader transcends the traditional boundaries of leadership. Change leadership is the catalyst that converts challenges into opportunities and uncertainty into innovation. It involves more than just responding to external shifts; it's about proactively shaping the organization's future. Leaders in this space don't just react to market dynamics, technological advancements, and societal shifts; they anticipate and influence them.

The impact of change leadership is profound and far-reaching. It affects every aspect of an organization, from strategic planning to operational execution, from organizational culture to customer engagement. Effective change leaders possess the vision to foresee upcoming trends and the agility to pivot strategies in response. They foster a culture of resilience and adaptability, creating an environment where innovation is not just encouraged but is a natural outcome of the organization's ethos.

Change leadership is pivotal in navigating the complexities of the modern market. With rapidly evolving technologies, changing consumer behaviors, and shifting global economics, organizations need leaders who are not just tech-savvy or market-aware but are also capable of leading teams through these transformations. They must balance technical knowledge with emotional intelligence, ensuring their teams are motivated, engaged, and aligned with the organization's vision.

We will also dive into the core attributes of effective change leadership. We explore the skills and mindsets that set apart successful change leaders. This includes their ability to communicate a clear vision, foster collaboration, and create a sense of shared purpose. We also examine the practices and strategies that help leaders to drive transformation within their organizations. We will explore real-world examples where effective change leadership has led to significant organizational transformations. These case studies will provide insights into how leaders have navigated complex changes, overcame challenges, and harnessed opportunities to create sustainable, long-term success.

The transformative power of change leadership lies in its ability to turn vision into action and ideas into reality. We aim to equip current and aspiring leaders with the knowledge and tools necessary to lead change effectively, not just as a response to external pressures but as a proactive strategy for growth and innovation. In doing so, we prepare them to be architects of the future, shaping their organizations to thrive in an ever-changing world. In the modern business ecosystem, understanding the forces that drive organizational change is paramount. These forces, both internal and external, compel organizations to continually adapt and evolve to maintain relevance and competitiveness.

One of the most significant external factors is the ever-changing global market trends. The global market is an intricate web of interconnected economies and industries, where a shift in one part can have far-reaching implications. Factors such as emerging markets, economic volatility, evolving trade policies, and global crises shape business strategies. Organizations must be attuned to these trends, understanding their impact on supply chains, consumer demand, and the competitive landscape. This global awareness enables proactive adaptation of strategies to align with these shifts.

Technological evolution stands as a pivotal driver of change within organizations. The rapid advancements in fields like artificial intelligence, cloud computing, big data, and the Internet of Things redefine operational norms. While offering opportunities for efficiency and innovation, these technological shifts also demand new skills, updated infrastructure, and robust cybersecurity measures. Constant technological assessment and adaptation are crucial for businesses to harness these advancements effectively. Another critical factor is the shift in customer behavior and preferences. Driven by demographic changes, cultural trends, and the digital information era, consumer expectations are constantly evolving. This necessitates that businesses remain agile, adapting their offerings, marketing strategies, and customer service approaches to meet these changing needs. Understanding and responding to customer behavior shifts is essential for developing relevant and appealing products and services.

Regulatory changes present both challenges and opportunities for organizations. The evolving landscape of industry regulations and standards can significantly impact various aspects of business operations. From product development to data management, organizations must stay abreast of these changes, ensuring compliance while also exploring opportunities these regulations might present for innovation or market differentiation.

Recognizing and understanding these driving forces of change – global market trends, technological evolution, customer behavior shifts, and regulatory changes – are critical for leaders. This knowledge allows them to anticipate changes, prepare their organizations accordingly, and transform potential challenges into opportunities for growth and innovation. This section not only highlights these forces but also aims to provide leaders with the necessary insights and tools to effectively analyze and respond to the dynamic business environment.

In a world where change is relentless and rapid, resisting it carries significant risks and negative implications. For organizations that fail to adapt, the consequences can be severe, impacting not just their immediate operations but also their long-term viability and role in the broader societal and environmental context.

One of the most immediate and tangible consequences of resisting change is the loss of market share. In today's competitive business environment, customers have more options than ever before. They are drawn to businesses that are innovative, responsive, and in tune with current trends. Organizations that cling to outdated models, technologies, or practices risk losing their customer base to more agile and forward-thinking competitors. This loss of market share can be a critical blow, often leading to a downward spiral from which recovery is challenging. Another significant repercussion of resisting change is decreased relevance. In an ever-evolving market, what worked yesterday might not work today or tomorrow. Technologies become obsolete, consumer preferences shift, and new regulatory requirements emerge. Organizations that are not prepared to evolve in tandem with these changes risk becoming irrelevant. This decrease in relevance can lead to a loss of brand value and reputation, making it increasingly difficult to attract and retain both customers and top talent.

The impact of resistance to change extends beyond organizational boundaries. There are broader societal and environmental implications to consider. In an age where social responsibility and sustainability are increasingly important, organizations that ignore these aspects in favor of maintaining the status quo may face not only a public backlash but also regulatory repercussions. This can further erode public trust and corporate legitimacy.

Resistance to change can also stifle innovation and growth within an organization. It creates an environment that is risk-averse and complacent, where new ideas are not encouraged or explored. This not only limits the organization's potential for growth and improvement but can also lead to a demotivated workforce, as employees seek environments where their creativity and innovation are valued and nurtured. The consequences of resisting change can be far-reaching and multifaceted. From losing market share and relevance to impacting societal perception and stifling internal innovation, the risks of not adapting are significant. This section of the book underscores the importance of embracing change, not just as a survival strategy but as a means to thrive and maintain a meaningful, responsible, and sustainable presence in the market and society at large.

This book is an invitation to embark on a transformative path, one that promises to challenge and enlighten, equipping you with the knowledge and tools necessary for effective change leadership in today's dynamic world. The journey ahead is designed to be both thought-provoking and practical, offering insights and strategies that are immediately applicable. We will delve into the nuances of leading change in various organizational contexts, exploring both the theoretical underpinnings and the practical applications of change leadership. Each chapter is crafted to build upon the last, creating a cohesive narrative that brings clarity and depth to the complex subject of change management.

Throughout this journey, we will explore the characteristics of successful change leaders, the strategies that have proven effective in different scenarios, and the common pitfalls to avoid. You will gain insight into how to foster a culture that embraces change, how to navigate through resistance, and how to sustain momentum in the face of challenges.

We will also look at real-world examples, drawing lessons from both successes and failures in change initiatives across various industries. These case studies will provide a rich context for understanding the principles of change leadership and will serve as a source of inspiration and learning. This journey is not just about acquiring new knowledge; it's also about self-discovery and personal growth. As you progress through the book, you will be encouraged to reflect on your own experiences and leadership style, identifying areas for development and strategies to enhance your effectiveness as a change leader.

By the end of this book, you will not only understand the intricacies of leading change but also be equipped with a set of practical tools and strategies to apply in your own organizational context. Whether you are a seasoned executive, an aspiring leader, or a professional keen on understanding the dynamics of organizational change, this journey will provide you with valuable insights and skills. So, as we embark on this transformative journey together, keep an open mind, be prepared to challenge your assumptions, and be ready to embrace the lessons that await. The path of change leadership is as rewarding as it is challenging, and it is one that is essential for the growth and success of any organization in today's ever-changing world.

Chapter 1: The Change Imperative

In the modern business landscape, understanding the urgency of change is critical for organizations to thrive. This necessity stems not merely from a desire to stay competitive but also from the fundamental need to adapt to an ever-evolving environment. Change, in the context of modern organizations, is driven by a multitude of factors, each exerting pressure that cannot be ignored.

Technological advancements represent one of the most significant drivers of change. The digital era has transformed the way businesses operate, from automating processes to leveraging big data for strategic decisions. Organizations that fail to embrace digital transformation risk falling behind, as competitors harness these technologies to enhance efficiency, customer experience, and innovation. Global market dynamics are another critical driver. The globalization of the economy means that businesses are now part of a complex, interconnected system. Changes in one part of the world can have ripple effects globally, affecting supply chains, market demands, and competitive landscapes. Organizations must be nimble and adaptable, ready to respond to these global shifts to maintain their market position.

Consumer behavior and expectations are also changing at an unprecedented pace. The digital age has empowered customers with more information and choices than ever before. Businesses must constantly innovate and align their products and services with evolving customer preferences and values. Failing to do so can lead to a loss of relevance and customer loyalty. Regulatory changes also necessitate organizational change. As governments and international bodies introduce new regulations to address concerns such as data privacy, environmental impact, and ethical practices, businesses must adapt their operations to comply. These changes often require significant adjustments in processes, policies, and systems. The workforce itself is changing, with new generations bringing different expectations and values into the workplace. This shift demands changes in organizational culture, leadership styles, and work environments to attract and retain talent.

The urgency of change in modern organizations is not just about responding to external pressures. It's about proactively seeking opportunities to innovate, grow, and lead. Organizations that understand and embrace this urgency are better positioned to navigate the complexities of the modern business world. They can turn challenges into opportunities, adapting and evolving in ways that ensure long-term success and sustainability. Embracing change as a constant requires a significant shift in mindset at all levels of an organization. It involves moving away from viewing change as a series of isolated events to be managed, and instead, seeing it as an ongoing process that offers opportunities for innovation, growth, and competitive advantage. This perspective encourages organizations to be proactive rather than reactive, to anticipate and prepare for change rather than simply responding to it. In a world where change is constant, adaptability becomes a core organizational competency. Businesses must develop the agility to pivot quickly in response to new information, market trends, and technological developments. This agility is not just about speed; it's about being strategic, thoughtful, and intentional in how change is approached and managed.

A culture that embraces change is one that values flexibility, learning, and innovation. It fosters an environment where experimentation and calculated risk-taking are encouraged, where failure is seen as a learning opportunity, and where employees at all levels are empowered to contribute ideas and drive improvement. In such a culture, change is not something to be feared or resisted, but embraced as a pathway to new possibilities. Leaders play a critical role in fostering this culture of change. They must lead by example, demonstrating a willingness to embrace new ideas, challenge the status quo, and adapt their leadership style to changing circumstances. Effective leaders in a change-centric environment are those who can inspire confidence, communicate a clear vision for the future, and motivate their teams to embrace and drive change. Embracing change as a constant also requires a strategic approach to organizational design and processes. This may involve implementing flexible structures that can adapt to changing needs, investing in ongoing training and development to build a change-capable workforce, and leveraging technology to support innovation and efficiency.

Recognizing the forces driving the need for organizational change is critical for businesses to remain competitive and relevant in a rapidly evolving landscape. These forces are multifaceted, stemming from both internal and external sources, and they significantly influence how organizations operate and strategize. Understanding these drivers is essential for effective change management and long-term success.

1. Technological Advancements: One of the most prominent drivers of change in today's business environment is technology. The rapid pace of technological innovation has revolutionized industries, leading to new business models, operational efficiencies, and customer engagement strategies. Organizations must adapt to these technological changes to stay ahead, whether it's adopting new software solutions, leveraging data analytics, or integrating artificial intelligence into their processes.

2. Globalization: The expansion of global markets has increased competition and created new opportunities. Businesses are no longer confined to local markets; they can reach a global audience but also face competition from international players. This global landscape demands that organizations adapt their strategies to different cultural norms, market conditions, and regulatory environments.

3. Changing Consumer Preferences and Expectations: Modern consumers are more informed, connected, and empowered than ever before. They demand quality, convenience, personalization, and sustainability. Organizations must be attentive to these evolving preferences and expectations,

adapting their products, services, and customer experiences to meet them.

4. Regulatory and Compliance Changes: The regulatory environment is constantly evolving, with new laws and standards affecting various aspects of business operations. From data protection laws to environmental regulations, businesses must adapt their policies and processes to remain compliant, often requiring significant organizational changes.

5. Economic Fluctuations: Economic shifts, whether local or global, impact market conditions and consumer spending. Organizations must be agile enough to navigate through economic downturns and capitalize on upturns, requiring continuous reassessment and adaptation of business strategies.

6. Workforce Dynamics: The nature of the workforce is changing, with new generations bringing different expectations to the workplace. This shift requires organizations to adapt their work environments, culture, and engagement strategies to attract and retain talent.

7. Social and Environmental Factors: Increasing awareness and concern for social and environmental issues have prompted businesses to rethink their operations and corporate social responsibility strategies. Organizations are being driven to adopt more sustainable practices and contribute positively to society.

Recognizing these forces is just the first step. Organizations must respond proactively, leveraging these drivers as catalysts for positive change. This involves not only adapting existing practices but also reimagining business models and strategies to align with the shifting landscape. By staying attuned to these driving forces, organizations can navigate change more effectively and position themselves for long-term success in an ever-changing world.

In a world where change is relentless and rapid, resisting it can have significant and far-reaching consequences for organizations.

This resistance, often rooted in a reluctance to depart from familiar methods or a fear of the unknown, can severely hinder an organization's growth and lead to a multitude of setbacks.

One of the most pressing consequences of resisting change is the loss of a competitive edge. In a marketplace that is constantly evolving, organizations that fail to adapt can quickly find themselves outpaced by more agile and innovative competitors. This can lead to a significant loss of market share and a diminished position in the industry. Closely linked to this is the risk of becoming irrelevant in the market. As consumer preferences shift and new trends emerge, products and services that once met customer needs may no longer suffice. This decrease in relevance can lead to a shrinking customer base and a substantial decline in sales and profitability.

Operational inefficiencies are another major consequence of resisting change, particularly in the face of technological advancements. Organizations clinging to outdated systems and processes may suffer from reduced efficiency and productivity, leading to higher operational costs and putting them at a disadvantage in comparison to more streamlined competitors. The impact of resistance to change is not limited to external market factors; it also significantly affects internal dynamics, particularly employee morale and engagement. A work environment resistant to change can lead to frustration among employees, especially those who are forward-thinking and adaptive. This can result in increased staff turnover, loss of valuable talent, and challenges in attracting new, skilled employees.

Resistance to change can make an organization less attractive to potential investors. Investors typically seek dynamic businesses that demonstrate adaptability and potential for growth. An organization resistant to change may be perceived as a higher-risk investment with less potential for future growth.

In industries where compliance with regulations is crucial, resisting change can also lead to legal challenges. Non-compliance with new laws and regulations can result in legal penalties, fines, and a tarnished reputation, further impacting the organization's standing in the market. An aversion to change can mean missed opportunities for innovation. Change often brings new possibilities for creativity and development. Organizations that do not embrace change may miss out on the chance to explore new ideas, products, or services that could open up new markets or revenue streams.

The implications of resisting change in a fast-evolving world are significant, affecting nearly every aspect of an organization. From losing market share and relevance to experiencing operational inefficiencies and employee dissatisfaction, the risks are substantial. To remain viable and competitive in today's dynamic environment, organizations must not only accept change but actively seek and embrace it as an opportunity for growth, improvement, and innovation. Exploring the patterns and dynamics of change processes is a critical aspect of understanding how organizations evolve and adapt in response to internal and external factors. Change is not a random or chaotic phenomenon but often follows identifiable patterns and dynamics that can be studied and understood. This understanding is key to effectively managing and leading change within an organization.

Patterns of change refer to the common pathways or sequences that change initiatives typically follow. These patterns can vary depending on the nature of the change, the organization's culture, and external influences. However, there are general phases that many change processes go through, such as initiation, where the need for change is recognized; planning, where strategies and actions are developed; implementation, where the change is executed; and consolidation, where the change is embedded into the organization. The dynamics of change involve the forces and factors that influence how change unfolds within an organization. These dynamics can be complex, involving a multitude of elements such as leadership styles, employee attitudes, organizational culture, resource allocation, and external pressures. Understanding these dynamics is crucial for anticipating potential challenges and resistance, and for developing strategies that facilitate smooth transitions.

One of the key dynamics in any change process is the interplay between driving forces – elements that push towards change – and restraining forces – elements that resist change. Effective change management involves identifying and strengthening the driving forces while addressing and mitigating the restraining forces. Another important aspect is the role of communication in change processes. Effective communication can help in aligning stakeholders, clarifying visions and objectives, and reducing uncertainties and fears associated with change. Poor communication, on the other hand, can exacerbate resistance and lead to misunderstandings and conflicts.

Change also has a temporal dynamic. The pace at which change is implemented can significantly impact its success. Rapid changes can lead to shock and resistance, while overly slow changes can lose momentum and effectiveness. Striking the right balance in the timing and pace of change is a critical aspect of successful change management. Emotions and psychological responses also play a significant role in the dynamics of change. Understanding and managing the emotional journey that employees go through during change is vital. This includes addressing fears, building trust, and providing support throughout the transition.

Identifying recurring patterns in change initiatives is essential for understanding how change typically unfolds in organizations. These patterns, while not universal, provide a framework that can guide leaders and change managers in planning and implementing effective change strategies. Recognizing these patterns also helps in anticipating challenges and preparing for potential resistance.

1. Recognition of the Need for Change: Almost all change initiatives begin with the recognition that change is necessary. This could be triggered by external factors like market shifts, technological advancements, or internal factors such as performance gaps, workforce changes, or organizational inefficiencies.

2. Development of a Vision and Strategy: Once the need for change is acknowledged, the next step often involves developing

a clear vision of what the change will achieve and formulating a strategy to realize this vision. This includes setting goals, identifying key stakeholders, and planning the steps required to drive the change.

3. Communication of the Change: Effective communication is a critical pattern in change initiatives. This involves clearly articulating the reasons for the change, the benefits it aims to bring, and the impact it may have on different parts of the organization. Communication should be ongoing, transparent, and inclusive, addressing concerns and expectations from various stakeholders.

4. Mobilization of Support: Successful change initiatives typically involve mobilizing support from key stakeholders. This includes securing buy-in from top management, engaging change champions within the organization, and building a coalition of supporters who can help drive the change forward.

5. Implementation of the Change: The implementation phase brings the change to life. This often involves a series of actions or projects that are executed to achieve the change objectives. It requires effective management, coordination, and allocation of resources.

6. Managing Resistance and Challenges: Resistance to change is a common pattern. Effective change initiatives anticipate this resistance and have strategies in place to manage it. This includes listening to concerns, addressing fears, and providing support to those affected by the change.

7. Monitoring and Adjustment: Change initiatives typically require ongoing monitoring and adjustment. This involves tracking progress, evaluating the impact of the change, and making necessary adjustments to ensure the change is on track and achieving its objectives.

8. Consolidation and Institutionalization: Finally, for a change to be sustainable, it needs to be consolidated and embedded into the

organization's culture and processes. This often involves reinforcing new behaviors, integrating changes into everyday operations, and ensuring ongoing support and resources are available to maintain the change.

By understanding these recurring patterns, organizations can better navigate the complexities of change initiatives. It allows for a more structured and strategic approach to change, improving the chances of successful outcomes and long-term sustainability.

Understanding the fluid and evolving nature of change is essential in the modern business environment, where adaptability and flexibility are key to success. Change is not a static or one-time event but a continuous, dynamic process that unfolds in various, often unpredictable ways. This fluidity of change means that organizations must be prepared to continuously assess and adjust their strategies, processes, and behaviors to align with the shifting landscape. The fluid nature of change is characterized by its unpredictability. Even with careful planning and analysis, external factors such as market fluctuations, technological advancements, or shifts in consumer behavior can alter the course of a change initiative. This unpredictability requires organizations to remain vigilant and responsive, adapting their plans as new information and situations arise.

Change is evolutionary. It builds upon itself, meaning that each change initiative can lay the groundwork for future changes. What starts as a small, incremental adjustment can evolve into a significant transformation over time. This evolutionary aspect highlights the importance of viewing change as part of a long-term strategy rather than a series of disconnected responses to immediate challenges.

The evolving nature of change also implies that what worked in the past may not be effective in the present or future. Organizations must therefore foster a culture of continuous learning and development. This involves encouraging experimentation, staying abreast of industry trends and innovations, and being willing to challenge and refine established practices. The fluidity of change impacts the entire organization. It's not confined to specific departments or functions but can ripple through the entire structure, affecting everything from high-level strategy to day-to-day operations. This widespread impact requires a holistic approach to change management, considering the interdependencies and potential effects across the entire organization.

In navigating the fluid and evolving nature of change, it's also crucial to manage the emotional and psychological aspects. Change can be unsettling for employees, and successful change management must address these human elements, offering support, clear communication, and involvement in the change process.

The first step in navigating change dynamics is recognizing that change is multifaceted. It often involves simultaneous shifts in various parts of the organization, including technology, processes, people, and culture. Each of these aspects interacts with and influences the others, creating a complex web of change that must be managed holistically. Organizational culture plays a significant role in how change is navigated. Cultures that are adaptable, open to experimentation, and tolerant of failure tend to navigate change more successfully. In such cultures, employees are more likely to embrace change initiatives and contribute constructively to their evolution and implementation.

Leadership is another critical factor in the dynamics of change. Leaders must not only initiate and guide change efforts but also be attuned to the responses of their teams. They need to communicate effectively, provide clear direction, and be responsive to feedback. Leaders also play a crucial role in setting the tone for how change is perceived and handled within the organization.

Employee engagement and communication are key to navigating the complexities of change. Change can be unsettling, and without clear, consistent communication and genuine engagement with employees, resistance may grow. Involving employees in the change process, considering their feedback, and addressing their concerns can help mitigate resistance and build a sense of ownership and commitment to the change. Another aspect is the pace and timing of change. Moving too quickly can lead to confusion and errors, while moving too slowly can result in lost opportunities and momentum. Finding the right pace for change requires a keen understanding of the organization's capacity for change and the external factors influencing the need for speed.

External factors such as market trends, economic conditions, and technological developments also shape the dynamics of change. Organizations need to stay attuned to these external forces and be prepared to adapt their strategies and operations in response. This often requires a balance between maintaining core strengths and being flexible enough to seize new opportunities. Navigating change dynamics effectively often involves dealing with uncertainty. Change can be unpredictable, and outcomes are not always guaranteed. Organizations and their leaders must be comfortable with this uncertainty and capable of making decisions in an environment where not all variables are known or controllable.

Analyzing real-world cases of both successful and failed change initiatives offers invaluable lessons for understanding the complexities of organizational change. By examining these cases, organizations can gain insights into effective strategies and common pitfalls, aiding them in navigating their change processes more effectively.

One prominent example of a successful change initiative is the digital transformation undertaken by Microsoft in the late 2010s. Under the leadership of CEO Satya Nadella, Microsoft shifted its focus from solely software to cloud computing and AI technologies. This change involved not only a shift in business strategy but also a cultural transformation towards a growth mindset. The success of this initiative is evident in Microsoft's rejuvenated product line, increased market value, and enhanced competitive position.

Conversely, a notable example of a failed change initiative is the merger of AOL and Time Warner in 2000. Touted as a revolutionary merger that would combine old and new media, it failed to achieve its goals due to a clash of corporate cultures, lack of clear integration plans, and the bursting of the dot-com bubble. This resulted in a staggering $99 billion loss in 2002 and the eventual spin-off of AOL.

Another successful case is the turnaround of LEGO in the early 2000s. Facing a dire financial crisis, LEGO embarked on a comprehensive restructuring process under CEO Jørgen Vig Knudstorp. This included streamlining operations, refocusing on core product lines, and embracing user-generated content. These changes revitalized the brand, leading to a significant increase in sales and profitability.

On the other hand, Kodak's failure to adapt to the digital photography revolution serves as a cautionary tale. Despite inventing the first digital camera, Kodak was slow to transition away from film, largely due to fear of cannibalizing its profitable film business. This resistance to change led to a decline in relevance and eventual bankruptcy in 2012.

These real-life cases highlight several key factors critical to the success or failure of change initiatives. In successful cases like Microsoft and LEGO, strong visionary leadership, clear communication, stakeholder engagement, and adaptability were evident. In contrast, the failed initiatives of AOL-Time Warner and Kodak suffered from poor planning, resistance to change, and an inability to effectively manage cultural and market shifts.

By studying these examples, organizations can glean valuable insights into the dynamics of change management. Success in change initiatives requires more than just a strategic vision; it demands careful planning, cultural sensitivity, and the ability to adapt to evolving circumstances. Understanding these factors can help organizations navigate their change initiatives more successfully, avoiding the pitfalls that have hindered others in the past.

Analyzing the root causes of failed change initiatives is critical for understanding the pitfalls that organizations often encounter in the process of change. This analysis helps in identifying common themes and mistakes, providing valuable lessons for future change efforts. Failed initiatives, while challenging and costly, offer rich learning opportunities that can inform more effective change management strategies.

One of the primary root causes of failure in change initiatives is poor communication. This can manifest as a lack of clarity about the reasons for change, inadequate explanation of the benefits, or failure to provide a clear vision of the future post-change. When communication is lacking or ineffective, it can lead to misunderstandings, mistrust, and resistance among employees. Another significant factor is insufficient leadership support and engagement. Successful change requires commitment and active involvement from the top levels of the organization. When leaders are not fully committed or fail to demonstrate their support, it can undermine the entire initiative. Leadership must be a driving force behind the change, providing direction, resources, and motivation.

Resistance to change is a natural human tendency and a common cause of failure in change initiatives. This resistance can stem from fear of the unknown, perceived threats to job security, or discomfort with new ways of working. Failure to anticipate and manage this resistance can derail the change process. Lack of stakeholder involvement and buy-in is another key factor. Change initiatives often fail because they do not consider the needs, concerns, and insights of those who are affected by the change. Engaging stakeholders early and throughout the change process is crucial for gaining support and valuable feedback.

Inadequate planning and resource allocation can also lead to the failure of change initiatives. This includes underestimating the time, money, and effort required to implement the change or failing to consider the complexities involved. Change initiatives need thorough planning and sufficient resources to be successful. Neglecting the cultural aspects of change is a common oversight in failed initiatives. Organizational culture deeply influences how change is perceived and implemented. Ignoring the cultural implications can result in a change that is superficial and not fully integrated into the organization's way of working.

Inflexibility and failure to adapt to evolving circumstances can contribute to the failure of change initiatives. Change is often unpredictable, and a rigid approach can make it difficult to respond to new challenges and learnings that arise during the implementation phase.

Positive experiences in change initiatives provide a blueprint for success. They offer insights into effective strategies, leadership approaches, and implementation tactics that resonate with the organization's culture and goals. For example, a successful digital transformation initiative might reveal the importance of comprehensive stakeholder engagement, effective training programs, and robust communication strategies. Organizations can analyze these successes to identify key factors such as leadership style, team collaboration, and resource allocation that contributed to their achievements. By emulating these aspects in future initiatives, organizations can replicate success and reinforce a culture of continuous improvement.

On the other hand, negative experiences, while often challenging and disheartening, are equally valuable for organizational learning. Failures and setbacks provide critical insights into what can go wrong in change initiatives and why. By conducting thorough post-mortem analyses of failed projects, organizations can identify flaws in their planning, execution, or adaptation processes. Common lessons from negative experiences include the consequences of inadequate planning, ignoring employee feedback, resistance to change, or misalignment with organizational culture. Understanding these pitfalls enables organizations to develop more robust strategies to mitigate similar risks in the future.

The key to learning from both positive and negative experiences lies in fostering a culture that values feedback and reflection. Encouraging open and honest discussions about what worked and what didn't, without fear of blame or reprisal, is crucial. This culture of learning should permeate all levels of the organization, with leaders setting the tone by openly sharing their own learning experiences and encouraging others to do the same. Documenting these experiences and the lessons learned from them is vital for organizational memory. This can be achieved through formal mechanisms like case studies, debrief sessions, and knowledge repositories. Such documentation ensures that valuable insights are not lost over time and are accessible to different parts of the organization.

The importance of change leadership stems from its ability to influence and shape the entire change process. Leaders set the tone for the change initiative. They are responsible for articulating a clear and compelling vision of the future that helps align the organization's efforts and objectives. This vision provides a sense of purpose and direction, making it easier for employees to understand the rationale behind the change and the benefits it promises.

Change leaders play a pivotal role in driving engagement and commitment among employees. They are instrumental in building trust and confidence throughout the change process. By demonstrating commitment, openness, and resilience, leaders can encourage a similar response from their teams. This is particularly important in times of uncertainty and disruption, where employee morale and motivation can significantly impact the outcome of the change initiative. Effective change leadership involves skillfully navigating the human side of change. This includes understanding and addressing the concerns and emotions of employees, managing resistance, and fostering a culture of adaptability and resilience. Leaders must be empathetic listeners and effective communicators, capable of conveying information transparently and addressing questions and concerns in a way that builds trust and clarity.

Another critical aspect of change leadership is the ability to make informed decisions in a complex and often ambiguous environment. Change initiatives rarely go exactly as planned, and leaders must be prepared to adapt their strategies in response to new information, feedback, and circumstances. This agility and flexibility are vital for keeping the change initiative on track and ensuring its relevance and effectiveness. Change leadership is not solely the responsibility of top management. It involves cultivating leadership at all levels of the organization. Encouraging a distributed leadership approach ensures that change is driven and supported broadly across the organization, enhancing its acceptance and integration.

Change leaders are responsible for crafting and communicating a compelling vision that clearly articulates the purpose and objectives of the transformation. This vision serves as a guiding light, providing direction and inspiration to the entire organization. It is the responsibility of change leaders to ensure that this vision resonates with employees at all levels, aligning it with the organization's values and goals. These leaders play a crucial role in developing and executing strategies that turn the vision into reality. This involves meticulous planning, resource allocation, and the implementation of effective change management processes. Change leaders must navigate through the complexities of transforming strategies into actionable steps while ensuring alignment with the overall vision.

Beyond strategic execution, change leaders are also instrumental in creating and sustaining a culture that is conducive to change. This involves fostering an environment where new ideas are encouraged, risks are taken, and learning from failures is seen as a pathway to innovation. They must build trust and buy-in among employees, encouraging openness to new ways of working and breaking down resistance to change.

The role of change leaders extends to being active listeners and empathetic communicators. They need to understand and address the concerns and challenges faced by employees during the change process. By maintaining open lines of communication and providing regular updates, they can alleviate uncertainties and build a sense of security and trust. Effective change leaders are adaptive and flexible. They recognize that change is not a linear process and are prepared to make adjustments in response to feedback and new challenges. Their ability to respond quickly and appropriately to evolving circumstances is crucial for maintaining momentum and ensuring the success of the change initiative.

Developing the qualities and skills of effective change leaders is essential for navigating the complexities of organizational transformation. Effective change leadership goes beyond conventional management skills, requiring a blend of strategic vision, emotional intelligence, and the ability to inspire and motivate others. Here are key qualities and skills that are crucial for effective change leadership:

1. Visionary Thinking: Effective change leaders have the ability to envision a future that is different from the present. They can articulate this vision in a way that is clear, compelling, and inspiring, helping others to see the potential benefits of the change.

2. Strategic Planning and Execution: Change leaders need to be adept at developing strategic plans that turn their vision into actionable steps. This includes setting goals, identifying resources, and outlining clear pathways for implementation. Equally important is the ability to execute these plans effectively, adapting as necessary.

3. Emotional Intelligence: The human side of change management is critical. Effective change leaders are emotionally intelligent; they are aware of their own emotions and can understand and empathize with the feelings of others. This skill is vital in managing resistance, motivating team members, and building trust.

4. Communication Skills: Clear, transparent, and consistent communication is key in change leadership. Leaders must be able to convey the vision, goals, and details of the change effectively to different audiences. They should also be skilled listeners, open to feedback and different perspectives.

5. Adaptability and Flexibility: Given the unpredictable nature of change, leaders must be adaptable and flexible. They should be able to pivot strategies in response to new information, challenges, or shifts in the environment.

6. Influencing and Persuasion Skills: Change leaders often need to persuade and influence a wide range of stakeholders, from senior executives to front-line employees. They must be able to build coalitions and persuade others of the need for change, even in the face of skepticism or opposition.

7. Resilience and Persistence: Change initiatives often encounter obstacles and setbacks. Effective leaders demonstrate resilience and the ability to stay the course despite challenges. They maintain a positive attitude and can bounce back from difficulties.

8. Collaborative Mindset: Change is rarely achieved in isolation. Leaders must be able to collaborate with others, leveraging the strengths and skills of different team members and stakeholders. This involves fostering a sense of teamwork and shared purpose.

9. Problem-Solving Skills: Effective change leaders are skilled problem solvers. They can identify challenges, analyze complex situations, and develop innovative solutions.

10. Cultural Sensitivity: Understanding and respecting the existing organizational culture is crucial. Change leaders should recognize the value of the current culture and seek to build on it, rather than attempting to replace it entirely.

Developing these qualities and skills can significantly enhance the effectiveness of change leaders. Training programs, mentorship, practical experience, and continuous learning are all valuable in cultivating these attributes in current and future leaders.

Setting the stage for the change leadership journey is an essential process that prepares an organization for the transformative steps it is about to undertake. This preparation is multifaceted, involving the cultivation of a shared vision, the creation of a receptive culture, effective communication strategies, and the empowerment of individuals at all levels of the organization.

The journey begins by developing a clear and compelling vision for change. This vision serves as a guiding light, articulating not only the nature of the change and the reasons behind it but also the benefits it will bring to the organization. Ensuring that this vision is shared and embraced across all levels is crucial for aligning efforts and intentions. Cultivating a culture that is open to change is another vital aspect of this preparation. This culture fosters an environment of innovation and open communication, where new ideas are welcomed, and employees feel secure in expressing their concerns and suggestions. Creating a culture that values adaptability and resilience is key to successfully navigating the challenges of change.

Effective communication plays a central role in setting the stage for change. Establishing open, transparent, and consistent channels of communication ensures that everyone is informed, aligned, and able to provide feedback. Regular updates and open discussions are instrumental in building trust and keeping everyone on the same page. Change leadership also involves identifying and empowering change agents within the organization. These individuals, influential and enthusiastic about the change, help drive the initiative deeper into the organization, acting as catalysts at various levels.

Before embarking on the journey, assessing the organization's readiness for change is critical. Evaluating current resources, capabilities, and the cultural and structural preparedness to undertake the transformation is an essential step in ensuring the organization is primed for change. The change process should be guided by a strategic plan that clearly outlines the goals, steps, and timeline of the initiative. This plan needs to be adaptable, allowing for flexibility in response to unexpected challenges and opportunities that may arise during the journey.

Providing training and support to employees is another key aspect of preparing for change. As change often requires new skills and knowledge, equipping employees with the necessary tools and understanding ensures they are active and effective participants in the process. Encouraging participation and fostering a sense of ownership among employees is also important. Involvement in decision-making processes promotes a sense of commitment and advocacy for the change, leading to more robust support throughout the organization. The journey of change is one of continuous learning and adaptation. Regular monitoring of the progress and effectiveness of the change strategies, and being willing to adjust the approach as necessary, is crucial for the success of the initiative.

Setting the stage for the change leadership journey involves a comprehensive approach that prepares the organization and its people for the changes ahead. It requires careful consideration of various factors, from creating a supportive culture and clear communication to strategic planning and continuous adaptation, all of which are crucial for a successful and sustainable transformation.

Chapter 2: Embracing the Change Mindset

Cultivating a mindset that welcomes change is a fundamental step in ensuring the success of any transformational effort within an organization. This mindset shift is about embracing change as an opportunity rather than viewing it as a threat or inconvenience. It's a perspective that recognizes change as an essential component of growth and innovation in the ever-evolving business landscape. To foster this mindset, it begins with leadership. Leaders must model the behavior they wish to see by embracing change themselves. They should exhibit enthusiasm for new ideas and approaches, demonstrating a willingness to adapt and learn. When leaders openly embrace change, it sets a tone for the rest of the organization, signaling that change is valued and expected.

Creating an environment that encourages open dialogue about change is also crucial. This involves establishing platforms where employees can express their thoughts, concerns, and suggestions regarding change initiatives. Such open communication helps demystify change and address any anxieties or misconceptions that employees might have. Providing learning opportunities that focus on the benefits of change, the skills needed to adapt to change, and the successes of past change initiatives can help build a more positive perception of change. Training programs that emphasize adaptability, problem-solving, and innovation are particularly effective in reinforcing this mindset.

Recognizing and rewarding flexibility and adaptability in employees reinforces a positive attitude toward change. When employees who are open to change and who contribute positively to transformation efforts are acknowledged, it encourages others to adopt a similar attitude. This can be achieved through formal recognition programs or through more informal means, such as positive feedback during meetings or team discussions.

It is also important to involve employees in the change process. When employees feel they have a voice in how change is implemented, they are more likely to buy into the change and support it. Involvement can range from participating in decision-making committees to providing feedback on proposed changes. Encouraging a mindset that views challenges as opportunities for learning and growth contributes to a change-friendly culture. When setbacks are seen as a natural part of the learning process, employees are more likely to experiment and take calculated risks, which are essential behaviors in times of change.

It's about building resilience. Change often involves uncertainty and setbacks. Developing resilience—the ability to bounce back from challenges and adapt to new circumstances—is crucial. This can be fostered through team-building activities, resilience training, and by creating a supportive work environment where employees feel secure in facing new challenges.

Adopting a change-friendly mindset in an organization holds immense significance, especially in today's rapidly evolving business landscape. This mindset is a key driver of adaptability, innovation, and long-term success. In a world characterized by constant change, whether in technology, consumer preferences, or competitive dynamics, a change-friendly mindset equips an organization to not just survive but thrive.

1. Encourages Innovation and Growth: A change-friendly mindset fosters an environment where innovation is not just encouraged but is a natural outcome. In such an environment, employees feel empowered to experiment, take risks, and explore new ideas. This leads to continual improvement, helping the organization stay ahead of the curve and maintain its competitive edge.

2. Enhances Agility and Responsiveness: Organizations with a change-friendly mindset are more agile and able to respond swiftly to market changes. They can pivot their strategies and operations quickly in response to new opportunities or threats, ensuring they remain relevant and competitive.

3. Builds a Resilient Workforce: Change often brings uncertainty, but a workforce that embraces change is more resilient and adaptable. Employees in such organizations are better equipped to handle transitions, adapt to new ways of working, and recover quickly from setbacks.

4. Drives Employee Engagement and Retention: A change-friendly culture is typically more dynamic and stimulating, which can drive higher levels of employee engagement. Employees are more likely to feel valued and invested in their work, leading to higher job satisfaction and lower turnover rates.

5. Prepares the Organization for the Future: A mindset that embraces change prepares an organization for future challenges and opportunities. By staying open and adaptable, the organization is better positioned to leverage emerging technologies, tap into new markets, and evolve its business model as needed.

6. Aligns with Evolving Customer Expectations: In a rapidly changing world, customer expectations are constantly evolving. A change-friendly mindset enables an organization to stay attuned to these changes and adapt its products, services, and customer experiences accordingly.

7. Cultivates a Learning Culture: Organizations with a change-friendly mindset often foster a culture of continuous learning and development. This culture encourages employees to acquire new skills and knowledge, which is essential for personal growth and the organization's ability to manage change effectively.

The significance of adopting a change-friendly mindset lies in its ability to create a forward-thinking, agile, and resilient organization. It enables businesses to innovate continuously, adapt to changes swiftly, engage and retain talent, and prepare for future challenges and opportunities. In a world where change is the only constant, such a mindset is not just beneficial; it's essential for survival and success.

Shifting from fear and resistance to embracing change as an opportunity is a transformative process, essential for organizations aiming to thrive in today's dynamic business climate. This shift is not merely a strategic adjustment but a fundamental change in the organizational mindset, turning perceived threats of change into avenues for growth and innovation. Understanding the root causes of fear and resistance is the first step in this transition. Fear often arises from uncertainties associated with change, concerns about potential loss, or apprehensions about the change's outcomes. Resistance, a natural response to these fears, is particularly pronounced when changes are introduced without sufficient communication or understanding of their purpose.

Effective communication is pivotal in overcoming fear and resistance. Leaders must articulate clearly why change is necessary, how it aligns with the organization's overarching goals, and the positive impacts it promises. This communication should be continuous and inclusive, creating a platform for dialogue where concerns and questions can be openly addressed. Involving employees in the change process can significantly ease resistance. When people are part of shaping the change, they are more likely to comprehend its necessity and lend their support. This involvement could range from soliciting feedback on proposed changes to actively including employees in planning and implementation phases.

Support and training are critical elements in facilitating a smooth transition. Providing the necessary training and resources helps employees acquire the skills and knowledge needed to adapt to the new changes, reducing anxiety and building confidence in their ability to navigate the new landscape. Sharing stories of successful change within the organization can also help alter perceptions about change. Highlighting instances where challenges were transformed into success stories demonstrates the potential benefits and opportunities that embracing change can bring. Cultivating an organizational culture that values adaptability, continuous learning, and innovation also plays a crucial role. In such a culture, change is perceived as an ongoing opportunity for professional growth and organizational advancement, rather than a sporadic or disruptive event.

Leadership is instrumental in this cultural shift. Leaders who embrace change, exhibit flexibility, and maintain a positive outlook during transformations set a powerful example for the rest of the organization. Their commitment to and enthusiasm for change can inspire a similar response across all levels, aiding in the shift from resistance to acceptance. Transitioning from a mindset of fear and resistance to one that sees change as an opportunity requires a comprehensive approach that includes clear communication, employee involvement, adequate support and training, sharing success stories, fostering a culture of adaptability, and strong, exemplary leadership. By adopting this multifaceted approach, organizations can transform the challenge of change into a catalyst for innovation and growth.

Fostering a culture that encourages a positive change mindset is pivotal for organizations navigating the complex and rapidly evolving business landscape. Such a culture not only embraces change but also sees it as an integral part of growth and development. Building this culture is a multifaceted process that involves redefining attitudes towards change, encouraging open communication, and creating an environment where innovation and adaptability are valued.

The process begins with leadership setting the tone. Leaders who exhibit enthusiasm for change and a readiness to adapt set a powerful example for the rest of the organization. Their attitude towards change, whether positive or apprehensive, can significantly influence the organizational culture. Leaders must therefore actively champion change, demonstrating through their actions and decisions that they value adaptability and innovation.

Open communication is another cornerstone of a positive change culture. This involves creating channels where information about changes is disseminated clearly and promptly, allowing for feedback and discussion. When employees are well-informed about the reasons for change and how it benefits the organization and themselves, they are more likely to view it positively. Additionally, providing platforms for employees to voice their concerns and suggestions makes them feel valued and involved in the change process.

Encouraging risk-taking and innovation is also crucial. In a culture that supports a positive change mindset, failure is not seen as a setback but as a learning opportunity. Employees should feel safe to experiment and propose new ideas without fear of repercussions if things don't go as planned. This approach encourages creativity and can lead to groundbreaking solutions and improvements. Training and development play a significant role in fostering a change-friendly culture. Providing employees with the tools and knowledge they need to navigate change effectively builds confidence and reduces resistance. This might include training in new technologies, workshops on adaptability skills, or seminars on change management techniques.

Recognizing and rewarding change-positive behaviors is another effective strategy. When employees who embrace change, adapt quickly to new situations, and contribute constructively to change initiatives are acknowledged and rewarded, it reinforces the value the organization places on these behaviors. Building a supportive community within the organization also contributes to a positive change culture. This involves nurturing a sense of teamwork and collaboration, where employees feel supported by their peers and superiors during times of change. A supportive community can ease the stress associated with change and make the transition smoother for everyone involved.

Fostering a culture that encourages a positive change mindset is about creating an environment where change is viewed as an opportunity, communication is open and honest, innovation and risk-taking are encouraged, training and development are prioritized, positive behaviors are rewarded, and a supportive community is nurtured. Such a culture is essential for organizations looking to thrive in an ever-changing business world.

Addressing concerns and resistance to change is a critical component of successful change management. Resistance is a natural human response to change, particularly when it disrupts familiar routines or introduces uncertainty. Effectively managing this resistance involves understanding its roots, empathetic communication, and actively involving those affected in the change process.

The first step in addressing resistance is to understand its source. Resistance can stem from a variety of factors, including fear of the unknown, perceived loss of status or control, lack of understanding about the change, or bad experiences with past change initiatives. Identifying the specific reasons for resistance in each case allows for more targeted and effective responses.

Empathetic communication is crucial in addressing concerns. It involves actively listening to employees' worries and fears and acknowledging their feelings. Communicating the reasons for the change, how it will benefit the organization and its employees, and the steps being taken to implement it can help alleviate anxiety and build trust. Transparency is key; people are more likely to support change when they understand why it is happening and how it will be managed. Involving employees in the change process can also significantly reduce resistance. When people are given a voice in how change is planned and implemented, they are more likely to feel a sense of ownership and commitment to the process. This involvement can take various forms, from soliciting feedback to including employees on change implementation teams.

Providing support and resources is another important aspect of managing resistance. This could include training programs to build new skills, counseling services to help employees cope with change, or clear guidelines and resources to help them adjust to new processes or systems. Addressing the cultural aspects of change is also vital. Cultural resistance occurs when change is perceived as conflicting with the organization's established norms and values. In such cases, it is essential to demonstrate how the change aligns with or enhances the organization's core values.

Leadership plays a crucial role in addressing resistance. Leaders must model the behavior they want to see, showing enthusiasm for the change and a willingness to adapt. They should also be visible and accessible, providing regular updates on the progress of the change and being open to feedback. Celebrating small wins along the way can help build momentum and demonstrate the benefits of the change. Recognizing and rewarding departments or individuals who adapt well to the change can encourage others to follow suit. Addressing concerns and resistance to change requires a combination of understanding, communication, involvement, support, cultural sensitivity, strong leadership, and recognition of progress. By addressing resistance proactively and empathetically, organizations can smooth the transition process and increase the likelihood of successful change.

Identifying common concerns and sources of resistance is a critical step in the change management process. Resistance to change is a natural human reaction, especially in the workplace where changes can impact routines, job roles, and the overall work environment. Understanding these concerns and addressing them proactively can significantly enhance the effectiveness and smooth transition of change initiatives.

1. Fear of the Unknown: One of the most common sources of resistance is the fear of the unknown. Change can disrupt the status quo, leading to uncertainty about the future. Employees may worry about how the change will affect their roles, job security, and daily routines.

2. Loss of Control: Change often comes with a shift in processes, roles, and structures. This can lead to a feeling of loss of control among employees who were accustomed to certain ways of working. The feeling of being powerless to influence the change can exacerbate resistance.

3. Concerns About Competence: Change may require new skills or knowledge, leading to concerns about competence. Employees might worry they don't have the necessary skills to adapt to the new way of working, or they may fear that the learning curve will be too steep.

4. Impact on Workload: The transition period during change can often lead to an increased workload. Employees might resist change due to concerns about added responsibilities or the effort required to adapt to new systems or processes.

5. Bad Experiences with Past Changes: If previous change initiatives were handled poorly, it can lead to skepticism and resistance to future changes. Employees might doubt the effectiveness of the new change based on their past experiences.

6. Lack of Trust in Leadership: Resistance can stem from a lack of trust in the leadership or the motives behind the change. If employees feel that the change is not in their best interest or that it's being implemented for the wrong reasons, they are more likely to resist.

7. Cultural Misalignment: Sometimes, the proposed change may not align with the existing organizational culture. If employees feel that the change conflicts with the core values and norms of the organization, they might resist it.

8. Social Dynamics: Resistance can also be influenced by social factors within the workplace. If key influencers or groups within the organization are resistant to change, their attitudes can affect others and create a broader culture of resistance.

Understanding these common concerns and sources of resistance is crucial for developing strategies to address them effectively. This understanding allows change leaders to empathize with employees, tailor their communication and support strategies, and involve employees in the change process, thereby reducing resistance and fostering a more positive attitude towards change.

Engaging with individuals' apprehensions effectively is a crucial aspect of managing change in an organization. Addressing these concerns requires a thoughtful and empathetic approach, geared towards understanding, communication, and involvement. Successfully engaging with apprehensions not only eases the transition for employees but also fosters a culture of trust and openness. Understanding and empathizing with employee concerns is the first step. Change leaders need to recognize that apprehensions and resistance are natural reactions. Actively listening to employee concerns and validating their feelings can go a long way in building trust. This understanding creates a foundation for more open and honest dialogue.

Clear and transparent communication is essential. Providing as much information as possible about the change, including the reasons behind it, the benefits it aims to bring, and how it will be implemented, can help alleviate fears of the unknown. It's also important to communicate the change in a way that resonates with employees, linking it to their roles and showing how it aligns with their interests and the organization's goals. Involving employees in the change process can significantly reduce resistance. When employees have a say in how change is implemented, they are more likely to feel a sense of control and ownership. This involvement can range from contributing ideas in the planning stages to participating in implementation teams or feedback groups.

Offering support and resources is another key strategy. This could include training and development opportunities to build the skills needed for the post-change environment, counseling services to help employees cope with change, or mentorship programs to guide them through the transition. Fostering a positive narrative around the change can also help. Highlighting success stories, celebrating milestones, and recognizing employees who have adapted well to the change can create a more positive perception of the change and its benefits.

Leadership plays a critical role in engaging with apprehensions. Leaders should model the behavior they want to see, showing enthusiasm for the change and a willingness to adapt. They should also be accessible, offering regular opportunities for employees to share their concerns and ask questions. Providing feedback mechanisms where employees can voice their concerns and receive responses is important. Regular surveys, town hall meetings, and suggestion boxes can be effective tools for gathering feedback and demonstrating that employee concerns are being heard and addressed. Engaging with apprehensions in a thoughtful, empathetic, and inclusive manner is vital for the success of any change initiative. By understanding, communicating, involving, supporting, and responding to employee concerns, organizations can navigate the complexities of change more smoothly and effectively.

Building trust and transparency is essential in mitigating resistance to change within an organization. Trust is the foundation of any successful change initiative, as it fosters a sense of security and openness among employees, making them more receptive to change. Transparency, on the other hand, ensures that the change process is viewed as fair, honest, and inclusive. Together, trust and transparency create an environment conducive to successful change management.

To build trust, leaders must first be trustworthy. This involves consistently demonstrating integrity, reliability, and fairness. Leaders should be honest about the reasons for the change, its expected outcomes, and any challenges that might arise. Acknowledging uncertainties and being open about what is known and what is not helps to establish credibility. Effective and open communication is key to transparency. Keeping employees informed about the change process reduces rumors and misinformation, which can fuel resistance. Regular updates about the progress of the change, what to expect next, and how it is impacting the organization are crucial. Communication should be two-way, with leaders actively seeking feedback and listening to employee concerns and suggestions.

Involving employees in the change process also helps build trust and transparency. When employees have a role in shaping the change, they are more likely to trust the process and support the initiative. This could involve including employees in planning committees, focus groups, or feedback sessions. It gives them a sense of ownership and control over the change, which can significantly reduce resistance. Acknowledging and addressing the emotional impact of change is important in building trust. Change can be unsettling, and leaders need to recognize and empathize with the emotions that employees may be experiencing. Providing support, such as counseling services or stress management workshops, demonstrates that the organization cares about its employees' well-being. Consistency in words and actions is another critical aspect of building trust. Leaders should align their messages about the change with their actions. Any discrepancy between what leaders say and do can quickly erode trust.

Recognizing and rewarding employees who positively embrace and contribute to the change also fosters trust and transparency. It shows that the organization values adaptability and is committed to recognizing and rewarding those who support its goals. Demonstrating patience and understanding that trust and transparency take time to build is essential. Leaders should consistently reinforce these values through their actions and communication, creating a culture that values open and honest dialogue.

Building trust and transparency to mitigate resistance involves consistent and honest communication, employee involvement, acknowledgment of the emotional aspects of change, consistency in words and actions, recognition and rewards for supportive behaviors, and patience. By cultivating these elements, organizations can create a more receptive environment for change and reduce the likelihood of resistance.

Tailoring change strategies to individual preferences in change interactions is an approach that recognizes and respects the diversity of employee responses to change. This personalized approach is crucial in effectively managing change, as it addresses the unique concerns, motivations, and learning styles of different individuals within the organization. Understanding that each employee has a distinct perspective and reaction to change is the first step. Employees may vary in their adaptability, comfort with ambiguity, and perception of the change's impact. Some may embrace change eagerly, while others might be more cautious or even fearful. Recognizing these differences allows leaders to approach each employee in a manner that resonates with them personally.

Effective communication is at the heart of this tailored approach. It involves not only disseminating information about the change but also engaging in meaningful, two-way conversations. Listening to employees' concerns and questions and responding in a way that addresses their specific apprehensions, can make a significant difference in how the change is perceived.

Providing varied channels and formats for communication also helps in catering to different preferences. While some employees may prefer detailed written communication, others might benefit more from interactive sessions such as workshops or Q&A forums. Offering multiple ways to receive and process information about the change ensures that more employees are engaged in a manner that suits them best. Leaders and managers should also be trained to recognize and adapt to these individual differences. They play a crucial role in the day-to-day aspects of the change and are often the first point of contact for employees' questions and concerns. Equipping them with the skills to handle these interactions empathetically and effectively is key.

Incorporating flexibility into the change process allows for adjustments based on employee feedback and preferences. This could mean phasing in changes gradually, providing additional support where needed, or even revising certain aspects of the change plan in response to employee input.

Offering support and resources tailored to individual needs is another important aspect. Some employees might benefit from additional training or mentoring, while others might need more time to adjust to new systems or processes. Providing these resources demonstrates a commitment to helping each employee through the change. Recognizing and celebrating individual contributions to the change effort can reinforce a positive attitude towards the change. Acknowledging the efforts of those who are adapting well, especially those who were initially resistant, can encourage others to follow suit.

Tailoring change strategies to individual preferences involves understanding each employee's unique reaction to change, communicating effectively and in varied formats, training leaders, incorporating flexibility, providing personalized support, and recognizing individual contributions. This personalized approach can lead to a more successful and smoother change process, with higher levels of employee engagement and support. Recognizing that individuals have diverse responses to change is a fundamental aspect of effective change management. In any organizational setting, employees will vary in their reactions to change based on personal experiences, attitudes, and beliefs. This diversity in response is natural and should be anticipated and respected in the process of implementing change.

Some employees might view change as an exciting opportunity for growth and learning, while others may perceive it as a threat to their comfort and stability. This variation can be influenced by several factors including past experiences with change, personal resilience, fear of the unknown, concerns about competence in a new system, or even differences in understanding the reasons behind the change. Customizing communication and support to individual preferences is crucial in addressing these varied responses. A one-size-fits-all approach to communication can lead to misunderstandings and increased resistance. Instead, providing information in different formats and through various channels can help cater to different needs. For example, some employees might prefer detailed written communication such as emails or newsletters, while others may respond better to face-to-face meetings or interactive sessions.

Offering support tailored to individual needs can significantly aid the transition. This can take the form of additional training for those who need to develop new skills, one-on-one meetings for employees who need more direct support, or providing access to counseling services for those who find the change particularly stressful. Leaders and managers play a key role in recognizing and responding to these diverse reactions. Training leaders to identify and understand different responses to change enables them to offer the appropriate support. They can then act as mediators, providing reassurance, clarity, and guidance where needed.

Encouraging open dialogue is also vital. Creating a safe space where employees feel comfortable expressing their concerns and questions about the change can lead to more effective management of individual reactions. It also helps in identifying common concerns that might need addressing at an organizational level. Recognizing the diversity in responses to change and customizing communication and support accordingly is about acknowledging and valuing the individual experiences and needs of employees. By doing so, organizations can foster a more inclusive and supportive environment that facilitates smoother transitions and more successful change implementation.

Creating inclusive change strategies that resonate with all stakeholders is an integral part of successful organizational transformation. An inclusive strategy ensures that the diverse perspectives, needs, and concerns of all stakeholder groups are considered and addressed. This approach not only enhances the effectiveness of the change initiative but also builds a sense of ownership and commitment among those involved. To develop an inclusive change strategy, start by identifying all the stakeholder groups that will be affected by the change. This includes employees at all levels, management, shareholders, customers, suppliers, and possibly even the wider community. Understanding the specific impact of the change on each of these groups is crucial. Once stakeholders are identified, engage with them to gather insights and perspectives. This can be achieved through surveys, interviews, focus groups, or town hall meetings. Actively involving stakeholders in these discussions helps in uncovering their concerns, expectations, and suggestions regarding the change. It also provides an opportunity to communicate the reasons behind the change and the benefits it aims to bring.

Communication is a cornerstone of an inclusive strategy. Tailoring communication to the needs and preferences of different stakeholder groups ensures that the message is understood and accepted. For instance, the way you communicate change to employees might differ from how you communicate it to shareholders or customers. It's important to be clear, consistent, and transparent in all communications. Equally important is addressing the feedback and concerns raised by stakeholders. Demonstrating that their input is valued and, where possible, incorporated into the change plan, can significantly increase buy-in and reduce resistance.

Training and support are also critical components of an inclusive change strategy. Different stakeholders may require different types of support to adapt to the change. For employees, this might include skills training or mentoring programs. For customers, it might involve user guides or customer service support to navigate new products or services. Leadership engagement across all levels is essential for driving an inclusive change strategy. Leaders and managers should be visible and accessible, serving as champions of the change. They should embody the change they wish to see, providing guidance and support throughout the process. Monitoring and evaluating the progress of the change initiative is vital to ensure that it remains inclusive. Regular check-ins with stakeholder groups can provide insights into how the change is being received and whether adjustments are needed. Celebrating milestones and successes along the way can reinforce a positive message and demonstrate the benefits of the change. Recognizing the contributions of different stakeholder groups in achieving these milestones can further enhance their engagement and commitment to the change.

Creating inclusive change strategies that resonate with all stakeholders is about understanding and valuing their diverse perspectives, engaging them in meaningful ways, communicating effectively, providing tailored support, and continuously monitoring and adjusting the approach. By adopting these practices, organizations can ensure a more successful and sustainable change process that is supported and embraced by all those involved.

Leading with empathy and adaptability is increasingly recognized as a critical component in the realm of change leadership. The effectiveness of any change initiative often hinges on the leader's ability to understand and respond to the emotions, concerns, and needs of those affected by the change. Empathy in change leadership involves the ability to put oneself in the shoes of others, to understand their perspectives and feelings about the change. It's about recognizing that change can be unsettling, and different people may react to it in various ways based on their experiences, fears, and personal challenges.

Empathetic leaders are attentive to these varied emotional responses and tailor their approach accordingly. They acknowledge the concerns of their team members, validate their feelings, and provide support where necessary. This doesn't mean always agreeing with their viewpoints, but rather understanding them and considering them in the decision-making process. Empathy also plays a crucial role in building trust. When employees feel that their leaders understand and care about their concerns, they are more likely to trust them. This trust is vital during times of change, as it can help mitigate resistance and foster a more collaborative and positive approach to the transformation. Empathetic leadership helps in maintaining morale and engagement. Change can be disruptive, and without empathetic leadership, it can lead to disengagement and a decline in productivity. By showing empathy, leaders can keep their teams motivated and engaged, even through challenging times. Empathy also extends to how change is communicated. Empathetic leaders communicate change in a way that is clear, honest, and considerate of the impact it may have on employees. They ensure that communication is two-way, providing opportunities for feedback and discussion.

Adaptability is the other side of the coin in effective change leadership. It refers to the leader's ability to adjust strategies, plans, and behaviors in response to changing circumstances and feedback. Adaptable leaders are open to new ideas and different ways of doing things. They understand that change might not always go as planned and are prepared to make course corrections as needed. This flexibility allows for more effective management of the change process and increases the likelihood of its success.

An adaptable leader also recognizes the need for personal growth and development. They are open to learning from experiences and are willing to adjust their leadership style to suit the needs of their team and the demands of the situation. Leading with empathy and adaptability is essential in today's fast-paced and constantly changing business environment. Empathy allows leaders to connect with their teams on a deeper level, building trust and easing the transition, while adaptability ensures that they can navigate the unpredictable nature of change effectively. Together, these qualities create a leadership approach that is responsive, considerate, and effective in guiding organizations through change.

Navigating the emotional aspects of change, both for oneself and others, is a critical skill in effective change management. Change, even when positive, can evoke a wide range of emotions, from excitement and anticipation to fear and anxiety. Understanding and managing these emotional responses are essential for a smooth transition and the well-being of everyone involved.

For Yourself: Self-Awareness and Resilience

- Self-Awareness: As a leader, recognizing your own emotional responses to change is crucial. Self-awareness allows you to understand how your reactions and behaviors might impact those around you. It involves reflecting on your feelings about the change and the biases or experiences that may influence these feelings.

- Maintaining Balance: It's important to maintain a balance between optimism and realism. While a positive outlook can be motivating, being realistic about the challenges of change is necessary for preparing yourself and your team to face them.

- Resilience: Building resilience is key to navigating change effectively. This involves developing coping strategies for stress, such as mindfulness, exercise, or seeking support from peers or mentors. Resilience enables you to remain focused and effective, even when faced with setbacks or uncertainty.

- Continuous Learning: Embrace the learning opportunities that change brings. Viewing change as a chance to grow personally and professionally can help shift your perspective from apprehension to enthusiasm.

For Others: Empathy and Support

- Empathy: Understanding and empathizing with how others are feeling about the change is critical. This means actively listening to their concerns, validating their feelings, and acknowledging that their emotions are a natural response to change.

- Effective Communication: Transparent and consistent communication can help alleviate fears and uncertainties. Keeping everyone informed about the change process, the expected outcomes, and how they will be supported through the transition is essential.

- Encouraging Open Dialogue: Create an environment where employees feel safe to express their concerns and ask questions. Encouraging open dialogue helps in addressing issues before they escalate and demonstrates that you value their input and well-being.

- Providing Support: Offer support tailored to the needs of your team. This could include training to build new skills, workshops on managing change, or one-on-one sessions for those who need extra assistance. Recognizing and acknowledging the efforts of your team in adapting to change can also be a powerful motivator.

- Leading by Example: Demonstrate adaptability and resilience in your own actions. Leading by example can inspire your team and set a positive tone for the change process.

Navigating the emotional aspects of change requires a blend of self-awareness, empathy, communication, support, and resilience. By effectively managing your own emotions and supporting your team through theirs, you can foster a more positive and productive change experience for everyone involved.

Demonstrating adaptability and flexibility in the face of change challenges is a critical leadership skill in the modern business landscape. Adaptability involves a leader's ability to adjust their thinking, strategies, and behaviors in response to new information or changing circumstances. Flexibility, a related quality, refers to the willingness to alter plans and decisions as the situation evolves. Together, these traits enable leaders to navigate the complexities of change effectively and guide their teams through periods of uncertainty.

Leaders who embody adaptability view change not as a threat but as an opportunity for growth and innovation. They maintain a positive attitude toward change, even in challenging situations, and are open to new ideas and ways of working. Their ability to quickly assimilate new information and apply it effectively in decision-making is a hallmark of learning agility, an essential component of adaptability. Adaptable leaders are not afraid to experiment and innovate. They understand that trying new approaches and taking calculated risks are part and parcel of navigating change. This openness to experimentation is often accompanied by a willingness to learn from failures and to use these experiences to refine future strategies.

Flexibility in leadership is also about being responsive in decision-making. Flexible leaders make informed decisions based on current situations and are prepared to pivot or alter their approach when necessary. They recognize that different situations and team dynamics may require different leadership styles and are skilled at adjusting their approach accordingly. Managing uncertainty is another crucial aspect of flexibility. Leaders who excel in this area can maintain focus and composure, providing stability and confidence for their teams, even when outcomes are unclear.

In practice, effective communication is key to adaptability and flexibility. Leaders need to clearly and effectively communicate any changes in direction or strategy, ensuring that everyone understands their role in the new plan. They also encourage input from their team, creating a collaborative environment where diverse perspectives are valued. While being adaptable and flexible, leaders also need to maintain consistency in core values and objectives. This balance ensures that changes and adaptations align with the overall mission and goals of the organization, providing a steady course amidst the fluidity of change.

Adaptability and flexibility in leadership involve embracing change, being quick to learn, fostering innovation, making responsive decisions, adjusting leadership styles to fit the situation, managing uncertainty, and maintaining a balance between consistency and adaptation. These qualities, combined with clear communication and a collaborative team approach, enable leaders to navigate change challenges successfully, positioning their organizations for ongoing success and growth.

Chapter 3: The Change Leader's Toolbox

We now jump into the essential skills and competencies that change leaders must develop to successfully drive and manage organizational change. These skills enable leaders to not only initiate and implement change but also to inspire and guide their teams effectively through the transformation process.

A fundamental skill for any change leader is a deep understanding of change management principles. This includes knowledge of various change management models and frameworks, an understanding of how to apply these models in different contexts, and the ability to anticipate and mitigate potential challenges that may arise during the change process. Change leaders must be adept at strategic thinking and planning. This involves the ability to envision the future state of the organization, set clear objectives for the change initiative, and develop a strategic plan to achieve these objectives. It also requires the ability to think critically about the potential impacts of the change and to plan for various scenarios.

One of the most critical skills in change leadership is effective communication. Leaders must be able to clearly and persuasively communicate the vision, goals, and benefits of the change to stakeholders at all levels of the organization. This includes not only verbal and written communication but also the ability to listen actively and empathetically to feedback and concerns. Emotional intelligence is crucial for managing the human side of change. This includes the ability to understand and manage one's own emotions, as well as the emotions of others. Leaders with high emotional intelligence can build strong relationships, navigate difficult conversations, and foster a positive work environment, even during times of uncertainty.

Successful change requires collaborative effort. Change leaders must be skilled at building and leading teams, including selecting the right people for change initiatives, fostering teamwork and collaboration, and motivating and guiding team members towards the shared goal of successful change implementation. Change often involves navigating complex and unexpected challenges. Leaders need strong problem-solving and decision-making skills to identify issues, analyze information, and make informed decisions that keep the change initiative on track.

As change is often unpredictable, leaders must be adaptable and flexible. They should be open to new ideas, willing to adjust plans as needed, and able to respond quickly to changing circumstances. Resilience and perseverance are key competencies for change leaders. Change initiatives can be challenging and may face setbacks. Leaders need the resilience to cope with these challenges and the perseverance to continue driving the change forward, even in the face of adversity.

Chapter 3 focuses on the crucial skills and competencies that change leaders need to develop to effectively lead and manage change. These include understanding change management principles, strategic thinking, effective communication, emotional intelligence, team building, problem-solving, adaptability, and resilience. Developing these skills equips leaders to successfully navigate the complexities of change and lead their organizations through transformational processes.

Cultivating competencies such as communication, adaptability, and resilience is essential for change leaders to effectively steer their organizations through the complexities of transformation. These competencies are not just skills to be learned; they are qualities to be developed and refined over time, forming the backbone of effective change leadership. Communication is a cornerstone of change leadership. It's about more than just conveying information; it involves engaging in meaningful dialogues, actively listening to feedback, and articulating the vision and steps of change in a way that resonates with various stakeholders. Effective communication also includes the ability to empathize with others' perspectives and concerns, ensuring that all voices are heard and acknowledged throughout the change process.

Adaptability is another critical competency for change leaders. In the fluid landscape of organizational change, plans can shift, and unexpected challenges can arise. Leaders who are adaptable are not thrown off course by these changes; instead, they view them as integral parts of the change journey. They are skilled at thinking on their feet, adjusting strategies as needed, and finding innovative solutions to new problems. Resilience is the capacity to withstand and rebound from challenges and setbacks. For change leaders, resilience means maintaining focus and positivity even when faced with obstacles or resistance. It involves a certain level of tenacity and determination, a resolve to see the change through to its successful completion. Resilient leaders also foster this quality in their teams, building a culture where challenges are seen as opportunities for growth and learning.

Cultivating these competencies involves a combination of personal development and practical experience. It requires change leaders to be introspective, to constantly seek feedback and opportunities for growth, and to apply their learning in real-world change scenarios. By developing strong competencies in communication, adaptability, and resilience, leaders are better equipped to guide their organizations through the uncertainties of change and towards a successful future.

Learning from examples of successful change leaders and their skillsets is an invaluable part of developing as an effective change leader. By examining the qualities, strategies, and behaviors of those who have successfully navigated complex change initiatives, emerging leaders can gain insights and inspiration for their own leadership journeys. Successful change leaders often have a distinct set of skills and attributes that enable them to effectively manage and drive change. These include visionary thinking, the ability to communicate effectively, emotional intelligence, resilience, and adaptability. Visionary thinking is a key trait of successful change leaders. They have the ability to see beyond the current state, envisioning a future that is different and more advantageous for the organization. This vision helps to guide the direction of the change and serves as a source of inspiration and motivation for others.

Effective communication is another hallmark of successful change leadership. These leaders are adept at conveying the vision and rationale for change in a way that is clear, persuasive, and relatable. They are also skilled listeners, able to understand and address the concerns and feedback of various stakeholders. Emotional intelligence is critical in navigating the human side of change. Successful change leaders are empathetic and understanding of the emotional impact of change on employees. They are adept at building relationships, managing conflict, and creating an environment of trust and openness.

Resilience is a trait that enables leaders to withstand the challenges and setbacks that often accompany change initiatives. Resilient leaders maintain a positive and forward-looking attitude, even in the face of adversity. They are able to learn from failures and setbacks, using these experiences to strengthen their approach to change. Adaptability is also essential. The landscape of change can be unpredictable, and successful leaders are those who can adapt their strategies and plans in response to new information and changing circumstances. They are flexible in their thinking and open to new ideas and approaches.

By studying the examples of successful change leaders, aspiring leaders can learn how these skills and traits are applied in real-world situations. This might involve analyzing case studies, seeking mentorship from experienced leaders, or participating in leadership development programs. Learning from these examples provides not only a template for effective change leadership but also the inspiration and confidence to apply these skills in their own contexts. Leveraging instruments and tools for change initiatives is crucial in ensuring the smooth execution and success of any transformational effort within an organization. These tools and instruments vary widely, encompassing everything from project management software to communication platforms, and are essential for planning, implementing, monitoring, and communicating change effectively.

A key instrument in change management is project management software. These tools help in organizing, tracking, and scheduling all aspects of the change initiative. They provide a clear overview of tasks, deadlines, and progress, ensuring that every element of the change plan is on track. Features such as task assignments, timelines, and progress reports are invaluable for keeping team members aligned and informed. Communication platforms are another vital tool in change management. Effective communication is critical for the success of any change initiative, and platforms such as internal messaging apps, email, and collaboration tools like Slack or Microsoft Teams can facilitate this. These platforms allow for the swift dissemination of information, real-time discussions, and the ability to reach all members of the organization easily.

Data analysis tools also play an important role in change initiatives. They provide insights into how the change is impacting various parts of the organization, allowing leaders to make data-driven decisions. These tools can help in identifying trends, measuring performance against objectives, and gaining feedback on the effectiveness of the change efforts. Change management frameworks and methodologies, while not tools in the traditional sense, are instrumental in guiding the approach to change. Frameworks like ADKAR, Kotter's 8-Step Change Model, or Lewin's Change Management Model provide structured methods for planning and implementing change. These frameworks can be tailored to suit the specific needs of the organization and the nature of the change.

Training and development tools are also essential, especially when change requires new skills or knowledge. Online learning platforms, workshops, and seminars can be used to equip employees with the capabilities needed to adapt to new systems, processes, or ways of working. Surveys and feedback tools are crucial for gauging employee sentiments and reactions to the change. Regular surveys can provide valuable insights into how the change is being perceived, areas of resistance, and overall employee engagement.

Performance tracking and reporting tools help in monitoring the impact of the change. These tools can track key performance indicators, provide reports on progress, and help identify areas that need adjustment. Leveraging a range of instruments and tools is essential for effectively managing change initiatives. These tools support various aspects of change management, from planning and communication to implementation and monitoring, and are invaluable in ensuring the success of change efforts.

Integrating technology and resources effectively is a vital strategy in enhancing change processes within organizations. The thoughtful application of technology and the strategic use of resources can significantly streamline change initiatives, making them more efficient, impactful, and adaptable to the needs of the organization. The integration of technology in change management can take various forms, depending on the nature and scope of the change. Advanced software solutions, such as project management tools, can be instrumental in planning and tracking the progress of change initiatives. These tools offer real-time visibility into the status of various tasks and milestones, facilitating better coordination and decision-making.

Communication technologies play a crucial role in ensuring that all stakeholders are kept informed and engaged throughout the change process. Platforms like intranets, email, social media, and collaborative tools like Microsoft Teams or Slack enable consistent and transparent communication. They also provide forums for feedback and discussion, allowing employees to voice their concerns and suggestions. Data analytics and business intelligence tools are increasingly important in change management. They offer insights into how the change is impacting the organization, enabling leaders to make informed, data-driven decisions. These tools can analyze employee performance, customer feedback, and operational efficiency, providing a clear picture of the change's effectiveness. Incorporating digital learning and development resources is essential, especially when change initiatives require new skills or knowledge. E-learning platforms, virtual training sessions, and online workshops can provide employees with the necessary training without the constraints of traditional, in-person methods. Resource management tools are also critical in optimizing the allocation and utilization of resources during change initiatives. These tools help in ensuring that human, financial, and material resources are used efficiently and effectively, reducing waste and increasing the value of the change effort.

In addition to technological integration, aligning and leveraging other organizational resources is crucial. This includes aligning human resources practices, such as recruitment, training, and performance management, with the change objectives. It also involves ensuring that financial resources are allocated effectively to support the various aspects of the change initiative. The integration of technology and resources should be guided by a clear strategy that aligns with the overall goals of the change initiative. This strategy should consider the current technological capabilities of the organization, the readiness and skills of employees to adopt new technologies, and the long-term sustainability of the technological solutions implemented.

The integration of technology and resources in enhancing change processes involves the strategic use of project management tools, communication technologies, data analytics, digital learning resources, and resource management tools. This integration not only streamlines the change process but also ensures that it is effective, responsive to the organization's needs, and sustainable over the long term. Exploring the array of instruments and tools available for change management is essential for any organization seeking to navigate the complexities of organizational transformation. These tools and instruments provide the necessary support for planning, implementing, monitoring, and evaluating change initiatives. Understanding what is available and how to leverage these tools effectively can greatly enhance the success of change management efforts.

1. Project Management Tools: These are critical for organizing, tracking, and managing the various elements of a change initiative. Tools like Asana, Trello, or Microsoft Project can help manage timelines, assign tasks, and track progress. They provide an overview of the project and facilitate collaboration among team members.

2. Communication Platforms: Effective communication is key during change, and platforms like Slack, Microsoft Teams, or Yammer offer robust solutions for keeping everyone informed and connected. These tools support real-time messaging, file sharing, and collaboration, making it easier to disseminate information and gather feedback.

3. Data Analytics and Reporting Tools: Tools such as Google Analytics, Tableau, or Power BI can analyze large amounts of data to provide insights into the impact of change initiatives. They can track key performance indicators, monitor progress, and help in making data-driven decisions.

4. Employee Feedback and Survey Tools: Gathering feedback is crucial in understanding the impact of change on employees. Tools like SurveyMonkey, Google Forms, or Qualtrics allow organizations to conduct surveys, gather feedback, and gauge employee sentiment, which is invaluable for adjusting change strategies as needed.

5. Change Management Software: Specific change management software like Prosci's ADKAR Model, ChangeScout, or The Change Compass can provide structured methodologies and frameworks to guide the change process. These tools often include features for planning, execution, and monitoring change, along with resources for training and support.

6. Learning Management Systems (LMS): When change requires new skills or competencies, an LMS like Moodle, Cornerstone, or LinkedIn Learning can deliver the necessary training and development programs. These platforms can host a variety of learning materials and track employee progress.

7. Collaboration and Ideation Tools: For brainstorming and collaborative idea generation, tools like Miro, MindMeister, or Microsoft Whiteboard offer digital spaces where teams can collaborate creatively. These tools are particularly useful in the planning phases of change management.

8. Document and Resource Management Systems: Keeping all documents, resources, and guidelines accessible is vital during change. Systems like SharePoint or Google Drive can store and organize documents, ensuring that everyone has access to the latest information.

9. HR Management Systems: Tools like SAP SuccessFactors or Workday can help align human resources with change initiatives. They manage personnel data, track employee development, and can be used for communication and engagement strategies related to change.

10. Financial Management Tools: Tools like QuickBooks or Oracle Financials can be used to manage the financial aspects of change initiatives, tracking expenses, budgeting, and ensuring that resources are allocated efficiently.

The landscape of change management tools is diverse and rich, offering solutions for every aspect of the change process. From project management to communication, training, feedback gathering, and more, these tools can significantly enhance an organization's capacity to implement change effectively. Choosing the right combination of tools, aligned with the organization's specific needs and change objectives, is key to a successful change management strategy.

Selecting the right tools based on the specific needs of change initiatives is a critical step in ensuring the effectiveness and efficiency of the change management process. Each change initiative has unique requirements, and the tools chosen should align with the specific goals, scale, and context of the project. Understanding the scope and objectives of the change initiative is the first step in selecting the appropriate tools. This involves identifying what the change aims to achieve, the processes involved, and the stakeholders affected. For instance, a large-scale digital transformation will require different tools compared to a change in organizational structure or culture.

Assessing the existing infrastructure and capabilities of the organization is also essential. This assessment should consider current technological platforms, the skill levels of employees, and any gaps that the new tools need to fill. Selecting tools that are compatible with existing systems and that employees can easily adapt to will facilitate smoother integration and greater acceptance.

Considering the communication needs of the initiative is crucial. Effective communication is key to the success of any change initiative, so choosing tools that enhance transparency, facilitate real-time updates, and enable two-way feedback is important. The tools should cater to a diverse workforce and be accessible across various devices and locations. Analyzing the training and development requirements associated with the change can guide the selection of learning management systems or training platforms. If the change requires employees to develop new skills or knowledge, the chosen tools should support effective learning and knowledge retention.

Evaluating the need for data analysis and reporting will influence the choice of data analytics tools. If the change initiative requires careful monitoring of key performance indicators and outcomes, tools that provide comprehensive analytics and customizable reporting capabilities will be necessary. The budget is another important consideration. While it's essential to choose effective tools, they also need to be cost-effective. Balancing the cost with the expected benefits and ROI of the tools is a critical part of the selection process.

Involving a cross-section of stakeholders in the tool selection process can provide valuable insights. This can include IT professionals, project managers, employees who will be using the tools, and senior leaders. Their input can ensure that the tools selected meet the practical and strategic needs of the organization. Selecting the right tools for change initiatives involves a thorough understanding of the project's goals and requirements, an assessment of existing capabilities, consideration of communication and training needs, data analysis requirements, budget constraints, and stakeholder input. By carefully evaluating these factors, organizations can choose tools that will effectively support and enhance their change management efforts.

Balancing technical expertise with people-centric leadership is vital in the realm of change management. This balance ensures that while the technical aspects of a change initiative are efficiently handled, the human element, which is crucial to the success of any organizational change, is not overlooked.

Technical expertise is undeniably important in managing the operational and strategic aspects of change. It involves understanding the technicalities of the change, such as new systems, processes, or structures being implemented. Leaders with strong technical skills can ensure that the change is viable, aligns with organizational goals, and is executed efficiently. They are adept at dealing with the logistical and practical aspects of the change, solving technical problems, and making informed decisions based on data and factual analysis.

Focusing solely on the technical aspects can lead to a failure in recognizing and addressing the human side of change. This is where people-centric leadership plays a critical role. People-centric leaders focus on the needs, emotions, and motivations of the people involved in the change. They are skilled at communication, empathy, and emotional intelligence. These leaders understand that for change to be successful, it must be embraced by the people it affects. People-centric leadership involves actively listening to employee concerns, involving them in the change process, and providing the support they need to navigate the transition. This approach helps in building trust and buy-in for the change, which are essential for its successful adoption.

To balance technical expertise with people-centric leadership, it's important for leaders to:

- Develop and demonstrate empathy: Understand and consider the feelings and perspectives of employees affected by the change.

- Communicate effectively: Clearly convey the technical aspects of the change while also addressing its impact on people.

- Encourage participation: Involve employees in the planning and implementation process, valuing their input and feedback.

- Provide support and training: Help employees acquire the skills and knowledge required to adapt to the change.

- Foster a positive culture: Create an environment where employees feel valued, respected, and supported through the transition.

- Lead by example: Demonstrate a balance of technical and people skills in their actions and decision-making.

Balancing technical expertise with people-centric leadership requires leaders to not only have a firm grasp of the technical aspects of change but also to be attuned to the human elements involved. By achieving this balance, leaders can ensure that change initiatives are not only technically sound but also widely accepted and supported within the organization.

Recognizing the importance of both technical and people skills is crucial for effective leadership, especially in periods of organizational change. This dual focus ensures that while the practical, operational aspects of change are managed competently, the emotional and psychological needs of the people involved are also addressed and nurtured.

Technical skills are the hard skills required for specific tasks or industry requirements. They include proficiency in specific tools, methodologies, processes, or systems relevant to the change being implemented. Leaders with strong technical skills can ensure that the change initiative is grounded in a solid understanding of the practical realities and technical requirements. These skills are essential for devising strategies, problem-solving, making informed decisions, and effectively managing the operational aspects of the change. Technical skills alone are insufficient for successful change management.

People skills, often referred to as soft skills, play a critical role in the human side of change management. These skills involve the ability to communicate effectively, empathize with others, manage relationships, and inspire and motivate a team. They are crucial for understanding and addressing the concerns and emotions of employees, building trust, fostering collaboration, and creating a positive work environment. People skills enable leaders to connect with their teams on a deeper level, understand their perspectives, and engage them in the change process. This connection is vital for overcoming resistance to change, maintaining morale, and ensuring that employees feel valued and supported during transitions.

The best leaders are those who can seamlessly integrate technical and people skills. They are able to understand the technical aspects of the change and communicate them in a way that is accessible and resonates with their team. They can balance the need to meet technical requirements with the need to address human concerns, understanding that both are critical to the success of the change initiative.

In practice, this balance might involve translating complex technical information into clear, relatable messages, involving team members in decision-making processes, providing training and development opportunities to bridge any skill gaps, and actively listening to and addressing the concerns and feedback of the team. Recognizing the importance of both technical and people skills involves understanding that effective change management requires a blend of operational proficiency and emotional intelligence. Leaders who can combine these skills are better equipped to drive successful change initiatives, as they can manage the practical aspects of the change while also ensuring that their teams are engaged, supported, and motivated throughout the process.

Finding equilibrium between technical proficiency and interpersonal effectiveness is a key challenge for leaders, especially in environments undergoing change. This equilibrium is crucial because it allows leaders to manage the practical aspects of their roles while simultaneously fostering positive, productive relationships with their teams and stakeholders.

Technical proficiency encompasses a deep understanding of the specific skills, processes, and knowledge required for a particular role or industry. It includes the ability to use tools and technologies relevant to the job, understanding and implementing best practices, and staying updated with industry trends. Technical proficiency ensures that a leader is competent in managing the operational and strategic aspects of their role, which is particularly crucial during periods of change when new systems or processes might be introduced.

Interpersonal effectiveness, on the other hand, involves the ability to communicate, collaborate, and lead people effectively. It includes skills such as empathy, active listening, conflict resolution, motivation, and team building. Interpersonal effectiveness is essential for creating a positive work environment, managing team dynamics, and guiding employees through the challenges of change. It helps in building trust, resolving conflicts, and ensuring that team members feel valued and supported.

Balancing these two areas requires a conscious effort. Leaders must not only focus on maintaining their technical skills but also continuously develop their interpersonal abilities. This can be achieved through:

- Self-awareness: Understanding one's own strengths and weaknesses in both technical and interpersonal areas is crucial. This self-awareness allows leaders to identify areas for improvement and seek out training or mentoring as needed.

- Continuous learning: Staying current in one's field and continuously developing both technical skills and soft skills is essential. This can involve formal education, workshops, reading, or engaging in professional networks.

- Adapting communication styles: Effective leaders adjust their communication to suit the audience and context. This might mean explaining technical details in accessible language to non-expert team members or focusing more on the 'why' behind changes to foster buy-in.

- Delegation: Leaders should recognize tasks that require their specific technical expertise and those that can be delegated to others. Delegation not only frees up time for leaders to focus on their key areas of expertise but also empowers team members, helping to develop their skills.

- Feedback mechanisms: Implementing regular feedback channels can help leaders gauge how well they are balancing technical and interpersonal responsibilities. Feedback from peers, superiors, and direct reports can provide valuable insights.

- Reflecting on leadership impact: Regularly reflecting on the impact one's leadership style has on the team and the work environment can provide insights into how well the balance is being maintained.

Finding an equilibrium between technical proficiency and interpersonal effectiveness is about recognizing the importance of both aspects in leadership, committing to continuous personal development in both areas, and being adaptable and responsive to the needs of the team and the organization. This balance is key to effective leadership, particularly in dynamic and changing environments.

Creating synergy between technical expertise and empathetic leadership is about weaving together the precision of technical skills with the understanding and compassion inherent in empathetic leadership. This approach is increasingly important in modern organizational environments, where leaders are expected to drive operational excellence while also nurturing a supportive and inclusive workplace. Achieving this synergy starts with the empathetic communication of technical knowledge. It involves translating complex technical terms into language that everyone can understand, considering the diverse backgrounds of team members. Leaders with this skillset are adept at explaining technical concepts in a way that is both accessible and sensitive to the impact these concepts may have on the team's emotional and professional wellbeing.

In empathetic leadership, there is an acknowledgment that behind every technical task or project are individuals with varied skills, motivations, and personal challenges. Leaders who understand these individual differences can effectively guide their teams, enhancing team dynamics and overall productivity. This understanding extends to applying technical problem-solving skills to interpersonal issues, using analytical abilities to identify and address patterns in team dynamics or workflow inefficiencies. Leaders who continuously develop both their technical acumen and empathetic skills set a powerful precedent for their teams. This commitment to lifelong learning demonstrates the importance of balancing technical prowess with emotional intelligence and inclusivity.

The process of inclusive decision-making is also key in blending technical and empathetic leadership. By involving team members in technical decisions and valuing their diverse perspectives, leaders can make more informed decisions while also making their team members feel respected and heard. The leadership style in this scenario is adaptive, flexing between a focus on technical details and empathetic understanding based on the situation at hand, such as prioritizing quick technical decisions in a crisis or focusing on empathy during conflict resolution.

When faced with technical challenges, empathetic leaders consider not just the problem at hand but also how potential solutions will affect their team. They strive to find resolutions that are technically sound while also promoting the team's wellbeing and professional development. The fusion of technical expertise and empathetic leadership is about mastering the art of balancing operational proficiency with a deep understanding of team dynamics. It requires leaders to be technically skilled and emotionally attuned, enabling them to guide their teams effectively through challenges and create a positive and productive work environment. This balanced approach is crucial for achieving organizational goals and fostering a culture of collaboration and respect.

Navigating the intersection of technical and change leadership is an intricate task that demands a nuanced approach from leaders. This intersection is where the precision and knowledge inherent in technical expertise meet the dynamic and often unpredictable nature of guiding an organization through change. Leaders who successfully navigate this intersection are adept at managing not only the logistical aspects of change but also its impact on people and organizational culture.

Leaders are required to have a deep understanding of the technical aspects of the change, whether it involves new technology, processes, or methodologies. This technical understanding is crucial for making informed decisions, foreseeing potential challenges, and ensuring that the operational aspects of the change are feasible and well-planned. However, technical know-how alone is not enough. Leaders must also possess the skills to manage the human side of change. This includes understanding how the change will impact employees, addressing their concerns, and motivating them to embrace the new ways of working. It involves communicating the change effectively, building consensus, and fostering an environment of trust and support.

A key challenge at this intersection is balancing the focus on technical details with the need for empathy and flexibility. Leaders must be able to switch gears between addressing technical issues and attending to the concerns and needs of their team members. This balance is crucial for maintaining team morale and ensuring that the change is not only technically successful but also embraced by the people within the organization.

Another important aspect is fostering collaboration between technical experts and other stakeholders. Leaders at this intersection act as a bridge, ensuring that technical teams and other parts of the organization work together cohesively. This involves facilitating communication between groups, aligning goals, and ensuring that all voices are heard and considered in the change process. Successful navigation of this intersection also requires adaptability. Change is often unpredictable, and leaders must be prepared to adjust their plans and strategies in response to new information or challenges. This adaptability allows leaders to respond effectively to the evolving nature of change initiatives.

Navigating the intersection of technical and change leadership requires a leader to be well-versed in technical aspects while also being skilled in managing the human and cultural elements of change. It's about striking a balance between operational proficiency and emotional intelligence, fostering collaboration across different groups, and being adaptable in the face of change. Leaders who master this intersection are well-equipped to guide their organizations through complex transformations, ensuring both technical success and positive people outcomes.

Understanding the dynamic relationship between technical and change leadership involves recognizing how these two facets of leadership interact and complement each other in driving organizational transformation. Technical leadership focuses on the mastery of specific skills, processes, and knowledge pertinent to a particular area of expertise. It is about applying this expertise to achieve operational excellence and meet organizational goals. Change leadership, on the other hand, centers around guiding an organization and its people through transitions, addressing the human and cultural aspects of change.

The dynamic relationship between these two forms of leadership is pivotal in ensuring that change is not only technically sound but also well-received and integrated into the organizational fabric. Technical leaders bring a deep understanding of the specific changes required, be it in technology, systems, or processes. They are adept at identifying what needs to change, designing solutions, and overseeing the implementation of these technical aspects. However, the implementation of these technical changes can have significant implications for the people within the organization. This is where change leadership becomes critical. Change leaders focus on the human side of these transformations. They work to ensure that the technical changes align with the organization's culture, values, and people. Their role involves communicating the reasons behind the change, addressing concerns and fears, and building buy-in and commitment among employees.

A key aspect of understanding this relationship is recognizing that technical changes are not just a series of operational tasks but also involve shifts in how people work, collaborate, and engage with each other. Successful leaders in this space are those who can navigate both the technical requirements of the change and its human implications. They understand that for technical changes to be truly effective and sustainable, they must be embedded within the organizational culture and embraced by its people.

This dynamic relationship also emphasizes the importance of collaboration and communication. Leaders need to facilitate dialogue between technical experts and those impacted by the changes. This ensures that technical solutions are designed with an understanding of the real-world context in which they will be applied and that any concerns or suggestions from employees are taken into account. The relationship between technical and change leadership is about harmonizing the technical aspects of change with its human elements. It's about leaders who are proficient in their technical domains while also being attuned to and skilled in managing the emotional and cultural dimensions of change. This holistic approach is key to driving successful and sustainable change within organizations.

Developing strategies for effectively leading technical teams through change involves a nuanced approach that balances the specific needs and dynamics of a technical team with the broader objectives of the change initiative. Technical teams often have their unique cultures, ways of working, and professional languages, all of which must be considered when guiding them through periods of transition.

1. Understanding the Technical Team's Perspective: Start by gaining a deep understanding of the technical team's work, challenges, and how the change will impact their processes and workflows. Recognize the value of their expertise and involve them in discussions about the change early on. This approach not only garners respect but also ensures that their insights contribute to the success of the change.

2. Clear and Relevant Communication: Communicate the change in a way that resonates with the technical team. Use language and examples that are relevant to their work. Clearly articulate how the change aligns with technical goals and objectives, and explain the rationale behind decisions, especially when they directly impact the team's work.

3. Involving the Team in the Change Process: Encourage participation from the team in planning and implementing the change. Involvement gives them a sense of ownership and control over the change, which can reduce resistance and increase buy-in. It also allows for the pooling of diverse ideas and solutions, potentially improving the outcome of the change.

4. Addressing Training and Development Needs: Identify any skill gaps that the change might create within the team and provide the necessary training and resources to bridge these gaps. Professional development opportunities not only equip

the team to handle the change more effectively but also demonstrate the organization's commitment to their growth.

5. Fostering a Collaborative Environment: Encourage collaboration within the team and with other departments or teams impacted by the change. This can involve cross-functional meetings, joint problem-solving sessions, or team-building activities. Collaboration can break down silos and foster a more holistic understanding of the change.

6. Managing Resistance with Empathy: Be attentive to signs of resistance or discomfort within the team. Address concerns with empathy and understanding. Provide a space for team members to express their fears or apprehensions about the change and work collaboratively to find solutions or compromises.

7. Leading by Example: Demonstrate adaptability and resilience in your leadership. Be open to feedback and willing to adjust strategies if necessary. Your behavior sets a tone for the team, and showing enthusiasm and confidence in the change can inspire similar attitudes among team members.

8. Regularly Monitoring and Adjusting the Strategy: Change management is not a set-and-forget process. Regularly assess how the change is impacting the team and be prepared to adjust strategies in response to new challenges or feedback. Continuous monitoring helps ensure that the change remains on track and is effectively managed.

Leading technical teams through change requires a strategy that combines clear, relevant communication, active involvement of the team, attention to training and development needs, a collaborative environment, empathetic management of resistance, leading by example, and ongoing monitoring and adjustment. By adopting these approaches, leaders can effectively guide their technical teams through change, ensuring both the technical success of the initiative and the well-being of the team.

Finishing the chapter on bridging the gap between technical and change-focused roles within organizations involves synthesizing the key concepts and strategies discussed and providing a conclusive guide on how to harmonize these two critical areas effectively.

In organizational change, technical and change-focused roles often operate in different spheres. Technical roles are grounded in specific skills and knowledge related to particular functions or technologies. These roles focus on the practicalities of implementing change, ensuring that it aligns with technical standards and operational needs. Change-focused roles, on the other hand, concentrate on the broader impact of change on the organization, its culture, and its people. These roles are concerned with guiding the organization through the transition, ensuring that the change is understood, accepted, and embedded within the organizational fabric.

Bridging the gap between these roles requires a concerted effort to foster understanding, communication, and collaboration across these different domains. Leaders play a crucial role in this process. They must have a foot in both camps, understanding the technical aspects of the change while also appreciating its broader implications. Effective communication is key to bridging this gap. Leaders need to facilitate conversations between technical and change-focused teams, ensuring that each group understands the other's perspective and how their work intersects. This communication should be ongoing, with regular opportunities for joint planning and problem-solving.

Collaboration between these roles should be actively encouraged. Joint workshops, cross-functional teams, and collaborative projects can help break down silos, allowing for a more integrated approach to change. These collaborative efforts can lead to more innovative solutions, as diverse perspectives and expertise are brought to bear on the challenges of change. Training and development can also play a role in bridging the gap. Cross-training programs, where employees gain exposure to different aspects of the organization, can be particularly effective. This not only builds a more versatile workforce but also fosters empathy and understanding across different areas.

Change leaders should also focus on aligning the objectives of technical and change-focused roles with the overall goals of the organization. This alignment ensures that all efforts are directed towards a common purpose, minimizing conflicts and maximizing the impact of the change initiative. Bridging the gap between technical and change-focused roles is essential for the success of any change initiative. It requires leaders who can understand and communicate across different domains, foster collaboration, provide opportunities for cross-training, and align the objectives of all roles with the broader goals of the organization. By successfully bridging this gap, organizations can ensure that change initiatives are not only technically sound but also widely supported and effectively integrated into the organizational culture.

Chapter 4: Initiating the Revolution

In this chapter, the focus is on the crucial first steps of any change initiative: crafting a compelling change vision and strategy. A clear and inspiring vision is the cornerstone of successful change, providing direction and purpose. It articulates a desirable future state that motivates and aligns stakeholders around a common goal.

Crafting this vision requires a deep understanding of the organization's current state, its values, and its aspirations. It involves envisioning what success looks like post-change and how it will improve the organization. This vision should be ambitious yet achievable, striking a balance between realism and inspiration. Once the vision is established, the next step is to develop a strategy that will guide the organization towards this future state. This strategy should outline the key steps or initiatives required to achieve the vision. It involves identifying resources, setting timelines, defining key performance indicators, and establishing clear responsibilities.

The strategy should be detailed enough to provide a roadmap for action but flexible enough to adapt to unforeseen challenges or opportunities. It must consider the various facets of the organization, including its people, processes, technology, and culture, ensuring that the approach is holistic and comprehensive. A vital aspect of this process is communicating the vision and strategy effectively to all stakeholders. This communication should not only inform but also engage and inspire. It's essential to articulate the benefits of the change, addressing both the organizational advantages and the impact on individuals within the organization.

Involving stakeholders in the development of the vision and strategy can also be beneficial. This collaborative approach can provide diverse perspectives, increase buy-in, and encourage a sense of ownership among those who will be impacted by the change.

Crafting a compelling change vision and strategy is about painting a clear picture of the future and outlining a practical path to reach it. It requires a deep understanding of the organization, a forward-thinking mindset, effective communication, and a collaborative approach. This foundation sets the stage for the successful implementation of the change initiative, guiding the organization towards its desired future state.

The vision serves as a beacon, guiding and motivating everyone involved towards a shared future. It encapsulates the essence of what the organization aspires to become, post-change, laying out a compelling picture of the future. The creation of such a vision demands a deep understanding of the organization's current realities, its core values, and long-term aspirations. It's a process that requires not just foresight but also a thoughtful consideration of the organization's unique identity and its potential for growth. The vision should resonate with all members of the organization, from the executive team to frontline employees, making it a unifying force that drives collective effort.

A well-articulated change vision does more than just outline a desired end state; it ignites enthusiasm and commitment. It gives people a reason to embrace the change, providing clarity on why the change is necessary and how it will lead to a better future. This clarity is crucial in overcoming the inertia of contentment with the status quo and in combating resistance to change. An inspiring vision acts as a framework within which strategies and plans can be developed. It sets the parameters for what needs to be achieved and becomes a reference point for decision-making throughout the change process. Every strategy, action, and decision is aligned with this vision, ensuring coherence and consistency in the organization's change efforts.

Communicating this vision effectively is as important as crafting it. The vision should be conveyed in a manner that is not only clear but also evocative. It should be communicated through stories and examples that bring it to life, making it tangible and relatable for every individual in the organization. Involving stakeholders in the creation and refinement of the vision can also enhance its relevance and appeal. When people have a hand in shaping the vision, they are more likely to understand it, believe in it, and commit to it. This participatory approach fosters a sense of ownership and empowerment among those who will be instrumental in bringing the vision to fruition.

The pivotal role of a clear and inspiring change vision in initiating a revolution within an organization cannot be overstated. It is the foundation upon which successful change is built, providing direction, motivation, and a unifying purpose for the entire organization. This vision, when effectively communicated and embraced by all, becomes a powerful catalyst for transformative change.

Articulating a compelling change strategy is a vital step in ensuring the successful implementation of an organizational transformation. This strategy serves as a roadmap, outlining how the change will be achieved, the steps involved, and the methods used to facilitate the transition. The first step in developing this strategy is to align it closely with the change vision. The strategy should reflect the vision's aspirations and goals, translating them into actionable steps. This alignment ensures that every aspect of the strategy contributes directly to realizing the envisioned future. In-depth analysis and planning are crucial. This involves understanding the current state of the organization, the desired future state, and the specific changes needed to bridge this gap. The strategy should address various dimensions of the change, including people, processes, technology, and culture.

Risk assessment and contingency planning are essential components of a compelling change strategy. Identifying potential challenges, obstacles, and resistance upfront allows for the development of contingency plans to address these issues if they arise. This proactive approach minimizes disruptions and ensures the resilience of the change process. Effective communication plays a central role in articulating the strategy. The change strategy should be communicated in a clear, concise, and transparent manner, ensuring that all stakeholders understand how the change will occur, their roles in the process, and the benefits of the change. Communication should be ongoing, with regular updates and opportunities for feedback.

Involvement and engagement of stakeholders in developing the strategy can greatly enhance its effectiveness. Engaging employees, managers, and other key stakeholders in the planning process ensures that diverse perspectives are considered and increases buy-in and commitment to the strategy. Flexibility and adaptability are important characteristics of a compelling change strategy. While it is important to have a clear plan, the strategy should also be flexible enough to adapt to changing circumstances or new insights. This adaptability ensures that the strategy remains relevant and effective throughout the change process. Measuring progress and success is also a critical aspect of a change strategy. Establishing clear metrics and key performance indicators to measure the success of the change allows for ongoing evaluation and course correction as needed.

Articulating a compelling change strategy involves aligning the strategy with the change vision, conducting thorough analysis and planning, assessing risks, communicating effectively, involving stakeholders, maintaining flexibility, and measuring progress. These strategies ensure that the change process is well-guided, strategically sound, and capable of achieving the desired transformation.

In any change initiative, aligning the vision and strategy with the organization's mission and values is paramount. This alignment ensures that the change is not just a strategic shift but also a reaffirmation of the organization's core identity and purpose. To achieve this, it's essential to start with a clear understanding of the organization's current mission and values. This understanding provides a framework within which the change vision and strategy can be developed. The change initiative should reflect and reinforce what the organization stands for, ensuring consistency and authenticity in its approach to change.

Incorporating the organization's mission and values into the change vision involves translating these foundational elements into a future-oriented perspective. The vision should articulate how the change will enable the organization to better fulfill its mission and uphold its values. This approach helps in positioning the change as a natural and necessary evolution of the organization. The strategy for implementing the change should be developed with the organization's mission and values in mind. Every aspect of the strategy, from the processes and systems to be changed to the way these changes are communicated and implemented, should be consistent with these guiding principles. This consistency ensures that the change is not just operationally successful but also culturally coherent.

Engaging stakeholders in discussions about how the change aligns with the organization's mission and values can be beneficial. This engagement not only helps in refining the vision and strategy but also builds a deeper connection between employees and the change initiative. When people see how the change aligns with the organization's core values, they are more likely to embrace it. Communicating this alignment clearly and consistently is also crucial. Stakeholders should understand not just what is changing and how, but also why these changes are in line with the organization's mission and values. This understanding can foster a sense of purpose and motivation, making the change more meaningful to those involved.

Regularly revisiting and reinforcing this alignment throughout the change process is important. As the change initiative progresses, continuous alignment ensures that the change remains true to the organization's mission and values, even as adjustments are made to the strategy. Aligning the change vision and strategy with the organization's mission and values is crucial for the authenticity and success of the change initiative. It ensures that the change is not only a strategic endeavor but also a reflection of what the organization stands for, fostering a sense of purpose, coherence, and commitment among all stakeholders involved.

In the process of initiating significant organizational change, identifying and addressing concerns and resistance is a critical step. Resistance to change is a natural human reaction, often stemming from fear of the unknown, comfort with the current state, or perceived threats to personal or professional interests. Effectively managing this resistance is essential for the smooth implementation of change initiatives.

The first step in this process is to proactively identify potential areas of resistance. This involves understanding the perspectives of various stakeholders, from employees at all levels to management and external partners. Engaging in open and honest dialogues, conducting surveys, or holding focus groups can reveal concerns that might not be immediately apparent. Recognizing these concerns early allows for more effective management and mitigation. Once concerns have been identified, it's crucial to address them directly. This often requires clear, empathetic communication that acknowledges the validity of these concerns while also providing reassurance and information. Transparency about the reasons for the change, the benefits it aims to bring, and how it will be implemented can alleviate fears and misunderstandings.

Part of addressing resistance also involves highlighting the support and resources available to help stakeholders adapt to the change. This could include training programs, counseling services, or mentorship opportunities. Providing adequate support not only helps individuals navigate the change but also demonstrates the organization's commitment to their well-being. Involving stakeholders in the change process can also reduce resistance. When people feel that they have a voice in how change is implemented, they are more likely to feel a sense of ownership and control. Encouraging input and feedback, and where possible, incorporating this feedback into the change plan, can foster a sense of collaboration and buy-in. Another key aspect is to model positive behavior and attitudes towards the change from the top of the organization. Leadership commitment to and enthusiasm for the change can be contagious, setting a positive tone that can trickle down through the ranks. It's also important to monitor the ongoing impact of the change and be prepared to make adjustments as necessary. Regular check-ins and feedback mechanisms can help identify areas where resistance is still strong and where additional support or communication may be needed.

Identifying and addressing concerns and resistance to change is a multifaceted process that involves proactive identification of potential resistance, empathetic and transparent communication, providing adequate support and resources, involving stakeholders in the process, modeling positive attitudes towards the change, and remaining flexible and responsive to ongoing feedback. This approach not only eases the transition for those affected by the change but also increases the likelihood of successful and sustainable implementation.

In any change initiative, proactively recognizing and addressing concerns from stakeholders is pivotal for success. Anticipating and responding to these concerns early can prevent misunderstandings, reduce resistance, and build trust in the change process. Stakeholders, ranging from employees and management to customers and partners, can have varied and significant concerns regarding how the change will affect them. The process begins with actively listening to stakeholders. This involves creating opportunities for open dialogue, such as forums, surveys, or one-on-one meetings, where stakeholders can express their views and concerns. Such interactions not only reveal potential issues but also demonstrate the organization's commitment to transparency and inclusiveness.

Once concerns are identified, addressing them promptly and effectively is crucial. This requires clear communication that acknowledges the concerns and provides relevant information. It's important to explain the rationale behind the change, how it aligns with the organization's goals, and the expected benefits. Addressing concerns also involves providing detailed answers to questions and dispelling any misconceptions or rumors. In cases where concerns are related to potential negative impacts, it's essential to discuss the support and resources available to help stakeholders adapt to the change. This may include training, additional resources, or transitional support programs. By doing so, the organization demonstrates its commitment to ensuring a smooth transition for all affected parties.

It's also beneficial to involve stakeholders in developing solutions to their concerns. This collaborative approach can lead to more effective and practical solutions and increases stakeholder buy-in and engagement in the change process. Leadership plays a key role in this process. Leaders should model empathy and understanding, showing that they genuinely care about the stakeholders' concerns and are committed to addressing them. This empathetic approach can go a long way in building trust and goodwill. Continuously monitoring stakeholder sentiment as the change progresses is also important. Regular check-ins and feedback mechanisms allow for timely identification of new concerns that may arise, enabling the organization to address them quickly.

Proactively recognizing and addressing concerns from stakeholders involves active listening, clear and empathetic communication, providing support and resources, involving stakeholders in developing solutions, empathetic leadership, and ongoing monitoring of stakeholder sentiment. This proactive and inclusive approach not only helps in mitigating resistance but also fosters a positive and supportive environment for change. Addressing resistance to change effectively is a critical component of successful change management. Resistance is a natural response, often rooted in fear, uncertainty, or a lack of understanding. Tackling this resistance with empathy and clear communication can transform potential obstacles into opportunities for engagement and growth.

Empathy plays a central role in addressing resistance. It involves understanding and acknowledging the emotions and perspectives of those who are resistant to change. Demonstrating empathy means actively listening to concerns, validating feelings, and showing genuine interest in the viewpoints of others. This approach helps in building trust and rapport, which are essential for overcoming resistance. Effective communication is equally important. Clear, consistent, and transparent communication helps demystify the change process, dispelling fears and misconceptions. It's important to communicate not just the what and the how of the change, but also the why. Explaining the reasoning behind the change, its benefits, and its alignment with the organization's goals can help stakeholders see the bigger picture and understand their role in it.

Developing tailored communication strategies can also be effective. Different stakeholders may have different concerns and may respond to different styles of communication. Customizing the message and the medium to suit various groups ensures that the communication is as effective as possible. Involving resistant individuals in the change process can lead to more positive outcomes. This involvement can take many forms, from participating in decision-making to being part of a change implementation team. Involvement gives stakeholders a sense of control and ownership over the change, reducing feelings of powerlessness and resistance.

Providing training and support is another key strategy. Resistance often stems from a fear of not being able to adapt to the new ways of working. Offering training sessions, workshops, or mentoring can help build confidence and competence, reducing resistance. Recognizing and celebrating early wins and positive outcomes of the change can also help mitigate resistance. These successes provide tangible evidence of the benefits of the change and can serve to motivate and encourage those who are resistant.

Being patient and persistent is crucial. Change can be a slow process, and resistance may not disappear overnight. Consistently applying empathy and effective communication, while reinforcing the benefits and successes of the change, can gradually reduce resistance.

Addressing resistance to change with empathy and communication involves understanding and acknowledging emotions, clear and transparent communication, tailored communication strategies, involving stakeholders in the process, providing training and support, celebrating successes, and being patient and persistent. These strategies can help transform resistance into acceptance and engagement, paving the way for a successful change initiative.

In the initiation phase of any change initiative, building a foundation of trust and transparency is essential. This foundation sets the tone for the entire change process and significantly influences its success. Trust and transparency are key to ensuring that stakeholders feel respected, valued, and engaged, which in turn fosters a positive and open environment conducive to change. Building trust starts with leadership. Leaders must demonstrate integrity, reliability, and sincerity. Their actions, decisions, and interactions should consistently reflect the organization's values and the objectives of the change initiative. When leaders act in a manner that aligns with their words, it reinforces trust among team members and other stakeholders. Transparency is equally crucial during the initiation phase. This means being open about the reasons for the change, the expected outcomes, the potential challenges, and how these will be addressed. Transparency involves sharing information freely and proactively, ensuring that stakeholders have a clear understanding of the change process and their role in it.

Effective communication is a cornerstone of building trust and transparency. Regular, clear, and honest communication helps in demystifying the change process and reduces the fear of the unknown. It is important to establish communication channels that are accessible to all stakeholders and to encourage two-way communication, where feedback and concerns can be raised and addressed. Involving stakeholders in the early stages of the change initiative can also build trust. When stakeholders feel that their opinions are heard and valued, and when they see that their input can influence the change process, it builds a sense of ownership and commitment to the change.

Setting realistic expectations is another important aspect. Overpromising or glossing over the challenges can quickly erode trust when reality falls short of expectations. Being realistic about the challenges and potential obstacles, while maintaining a positive and solution-focused attitude, helps build credibility and trust. Acknowledging and addressing concerns and fears directly is also crucial. Ignoring or minimizing these concerns can lead to mistrust and increased resistance. Leaders should provide forums where concerns can be raised and discussed openly, and where honest, empathetic responses are provided. Demonstrating commitment to the well-being of stakeholders throughout the change process reinforces trust. This can include providing support resources, maintaining a focus on employee well-being, and ensuring that the change process considers the impact on people at every step.

Building a foundation of trust and transparency during the initiation phase of a change initiative involves demonstrating consistent and value-driven leadership, practicing open and proactive communication, involving stakeholders, setting realistic expectations, addressing concerns directly, and showing commitment to stakeholder well-being. This foundation is crucial for creating a supportive environment that facilitates successful change.

In the journey of initiating a revolution, the effective utilization of various instruments and tools plays a crucial role in laying a strong foundation for change. These tools are vital in planning, implementing, monitoring, and communicating the change, ensuring a systematic and organized approach. Project Management Software is indispensable for organizing the various aspects of a change initiative. Tools like Asana, Trello, or Microsoft Project help in tracking progress, managing timelines, and ensuring that tasks are completed on schedule. They provide a central platform where all the elements of the change process can be monitored and managed efficiently.

Communication Platforms are essential in maintaining clear and consistent communication throughout the change process. Tools such as Slack, Microsoft Teams, or internal communication networks facilitate real-time interaction, enabling quick dissemination of information and timely feedback. They play a key role in keeping everyone aligned and informed.

Survey and Feedback Tools like SurveyMonkey or Google Forms are critical in understanding the pulse of the organization. Regular surveys and feedback mechanisms provide insights into how the change is perceived by different stakeholders and help in addressing concerns proactively. Data Analytics Tools offer valuable insights into the progress and impact of the change initiative. Tools such as Google Analytics or Tableau help in measuring key performance indicators, analyzing trends, and making data-driven decisions.

Change Management Frameworks and Models provide a structured approach to managing change. Models like ADKAR, Kotter's 8-Step Process, or Lewin's Change Theory offer proven methodologies for planning and implementing change effectively. Training and Development Platforms are necessary when the change requires new skills or competencies. E-learning platforms, webinars, and online workshops can be used to equip employees with the knowledge and skills needed for the transition.

Collaboration Tools like Miro or Microsoft Whiteboard facilitate brainstorming and idea generation, enabling collaborative problem-solving and innovative thinking. Document Management Systems ensure that all relevant documentation related to the change initiative is organized and accessible. Platforms like SharePoint or Google Drive are useful for storing, sharing, and managing documents efficiently. The utilization of these instruments and tools in the initiation phase of change is integral to the success of the initiative. They bring structure, efficiency, and clarity to the process, enabling organizations to navigate the complexities of change with confidence and precision.

Leveraging specific instruments and tools during the initiation phase of a change initiative is crucial in laying the groundwork for successful implementation. These tools are tailored to address the unique challenges of starting a change process, ensuring that the foundation of the initiative is strong and well-planned.

Change Readiness Assessments are vital at this stage. Tools designed to gauge the organization's readiness for change help identify potential challenges and areas of resistance early on. These assessments can take the form of surveys, interviews, or workshops and provide valuable insights into the organization's preparedness for the upcoming change. Stakeholder Analysis Tools are used to identify and categorize the individuals and groups affected by the change. Understanding the influence, interest, and potential impact of various stakeholders is key to developing effective strategies for engagement and communication.

Visioning Workshops and Tools help in clearly defining and articulating the change vision. These interactive sessions encourage participation and input from various stakeholders, ensuring that the vision resonates across the organization. Communication Planning Tools are essential for devising an effective communication strategy. They help outline the key messages, communication channels, frequency, and target audiences, ensuring that the communication about the change is consistent, clear, and reaches all relevant parties.

Roadmapping Software assists in creating a detailed plan for the change initiative. These tools help visualize the timeline, key milestones, and deliverables, providing a clear path forward and ensuring that all aspects of the change are accounted for. Risk Management Tools are used to identify, assess, and mitigate potential risks associated with the change. By anticipating and planning for possible challenges, these tools help minimize disruptions during the change process. Collaboration Platforms facilitate effective teamwork during the change initiation phase. They provide a space for team members to share ideas, work on documents collaboratively, and maintain ongoing communication. Decision-Making Frameworks aid in making informed choices during the initial phases of the change process. These frameworks provide structured approaches to evaluate options, consider potential impacts, and make decisions that are aligned with the change objectives.

By leveraging these specific instruments and tools, organizations can effectively navigate the complexities of initiating change. These tools not only provide structure and clarity but also ensure that the change initiative is aligned with the organization's goals and is responsive to the needs and concerns of its stakeholders. In the initiation phase of a revolution, ensuring effective communication and collaboration is fundamental to laying a strong foundation for the change process. This phase is critical in setting the tone for how the change is perceived and embraced within the organization.

Effective communication during this phase involves clarity, consistency, and transparency. It's essential to clearly articulate the reasons behind the change, the goals to be achieved, and the impact it will have on various stakeholders. Consistent messaging across all levels of the organization helps in aligning everyone's understanding and expectations. Transparency is crucial in building trust; being open about the challenges and uncertainties as well as the potential benefits of the change helps in fostering a culture of honesty and openness.

Collaboration is equally important in this phase. It involves bringing together diverse groups within the organization to discuss, plan, and execute the initial steps of the change initiative. Collaboration ensures that a wide range of perspectives is considered, which can lead to more innovative and effective solutions. It also helps in building a sense of ownership and commitment among those who are involved in the change process. Creating platforms and opportunities for dialogue is a key part of facilitating effective communication and collaboration. This could be in the form of town hall meetings, workshops, focus groups, or digital platforms where ideas can be shared, and feedback can be gathered. These forums encourage participation and allow for two-way communication, where concerns can be raised and addressed.

Leaders play a pivotal role in this phase by modeling the way for effective communication and collaboration. By actively listening, being open to feedback, and showing a willingness to adapt, leaders can demonstrate their commitment to a collaborative and inclusive change process. Another aspect of ensuring effective communication and collaboration is acknowledging and addressing the emotional side of change. Change can provoke anxiety and uncertainty, and it's important for leaders to recognize and address these emotions. This might involve providing support resources, acknowledging the difficulties of transition, and celebrating early wins to boost morale.

Ensuring effective communication and collaboration during the initiation phase of a change initiative involves clear, consistent, and transparent communication, fostering an environment of collaboration, creating platforms for dialogue, leadership by example, and acknowledging the emotional aspects of change. These elements are crucial in building a strong foundation for the change process and in ensuring its successful implementation. In the crucial initiation phase of a change initiative, the strategic application of technology and resources plays a vital role in streamlining the process. This approach enhances efficiency, facilitates better organization, and ensures that all aspects of the initiation are addressed effectively.

Applying technology in this phase involves using digital tools to manage and coordinate the various components of the change process. Project management software, for example, can be used to create detailed plans, assign tasks, set deadlines, and track progress. These tools provide a centralized platform for monitoring all activities related to the change initiative, making it easier to keep everything on track.

Communication technologies are another key resource. Utilizing platforms such as email, instant messaging, and video conferencing can facilitate clear and consistent communication across the organization. These technologies ensure that information about the change is disseminated quickly and effectively, reaching all stakeholders regardless of their location.

Data analytics tools can be employed to analyze various aspects of the organization's current state and predict potential impacts of the change. This data-driven approach aids in making informed decisions and helps in anticipating challenges that may arise during the initiation phase. Collaboration tools are essential for fostering teamwork and collective problem-solving during the initiation process. Platforms that support document sharing, real-time editing, and virtual brainstorming sessions enable teams to work together seamlessly, even when they are not physically co-located.

In addition to technology, allocating the right human resources is critical. This might involve forming a dedicated change management team or task force, comprising individuals with the necessary skills and experience to drive the initiation process effectively. These teams play a pivotal role in planning, executing, and monitoring the various aspects of the change. Training and development resources are also crucial in preparing the organization for change. Providing training sessions, workshops, or online courses can equip employees with the skills and knowledge needed to adapt to new systems, processes, or ways of working.

Leveraging financial resources wisely is key to ensuring that the initiation phase is well-supported. This involves budgeting for the various costs associated with the initiation, such as technology investments, training programs, and human resources. Effective financial planning ensures that the necessary funds are available to support the initiation activities. Mobilizing teams and stakeholders for transformative action is a critical phase in the change process. This stage is about galvanizing the entire organization towards a common goal, ensuring that all involved are aligned, motivated, and prepared for the journey ahead.

The process starts with clearly communicating the vision and objectives of the change. This communication needs to be compelling, painting a picture of the future that is both desirable and achievable. It's important for everyone to understand not only what is changing but also why the change is necessary and how it will benefit the organization and its people. Engaging and involving teams and stakeholders in the change process is vital. Inclusion fosters a sense of ownership and commitment, as people are more likely to support a change that they have helped shape. Opportunities for involvement could include participatory planning sessions, feedback mechanisms, and role assignments in the change initiative. Leaders play a key role in mobilizing teams and stakeholders. They need to be visible, accessible, and actively involved, demonstrating their commitment to the change. Effective leaders inspire and motivate their teams, providing the support and resources needed to navigate the transition. Building a coalition of supporters and change champions can amplify the impact of the mobilization effort. These are individuals who are enthusiastic about the change and can influence their peers. They can act as role models, helping to spread positive messages about the change and addressing any resistance or skepticism.

Providing the necessary training and development is crucial to prepare teams for the change. This might involve skill development programs, workshops, or informational sessions to ensure that everyone has the knowledge and abilities required to adapt to the new ways of working. Recognition and rewards can also be powerful tools for mobilizing teams and stakeholders. Acknowledging and celebrating contributions and achievements, even small ones, can boost morale and reinforce the positive aspects of the change.

Regular and consistent follow-up is important to maintain momentum. Keeping teams and stakeholders informed about progress, challenges, and successes keeps the change initiative front and center, reinforcing its importance and maintaining engagement. Mobilizing teams and stakeholders for transformative action involves clear communication of the vision and objectives, engaging and involving people in the change process, leadership visibility and involvement, building a coalition of supporters, providing necessary training and development, using recognition and rewards to motivate, and regular follow-up to maintain momentum. These elements are critical in rallying the organization around the change and driving it forward with collective effort and enthusiasm.

Inspiring and motivating teams to embrace the change vision is a pivotal task in the change management process. It involves creating a shared understanding of the change and fostering an environment where team members are not only ready to accept the change but are also enthusiastic about contributing to its success. To inspire teams, it's crucial to communicate the change vision in a way that resonates with them. This means connecting the vision to the team's values, goals, and aspirations. When team members see how the change aligns with their personal and professional objectives, they are more likely to feel connected to the vision and motivated to contribute to its realization.

Engaging storytelling can be a powerful tool in this process. Sharing stories that illustrate the benefits of the change, or highlighting successful examples from other organizations, can make the vision more tangible and relatable. Stories help in painting a vivid picture of the future and can be more inspiring than abstract concepts or data. Leaders need to embody the change vision in their actions and behaviors. When leaders demonstrate their commitment to the vision, it sets a powerful example for the team. This commitment can be shown through decisions, actions, and the way leaders communicate and interact with their teams.

Creating opportunities for meaningful involvement is also key to inspiring and motivating teams. When team members have a role in shaping the change, whether through providing feedback, participating in planning, or being involved in implementation, they feel a sense of ownership and are more invested in the outcome. Recognizing and celebrating early successes can boost morale and motivate teams. Even small wins can be significant in building momentum and reinforcing the belief that the change is achievable and beneficial. Providing support and resources is essential to ensure teams feel equipped to handle the change. This includes training, mentorship, and access to information. When team members feel supported and know they have the resources they need, they are more confident in their ability to adapt and contribute. Fostering a positive and inclusive team culture is also important. A culture that values openness, collaboration, and innovation creates an environment where embracing change becomes a natural inclination rather than a forced directive.

Inspiring and motivating teams to embrace the change vision requires effective communication that connects the vision to team values, engaging storytelling, leaders who model the vision, opportunities for meaningful involvement, recognition of successes, provision of support and resources, and fostering a positive team culture. These strategies help transform the change vision from a concept into a shared goal that teams are eager to achieve.

Fostering a sense of ownership and accountability among stakeholders is an essential aspect of facilitating effective change. When stakeholders feel a sense of personal investment and responsibility towards the change initiative, it greatly enhances the likelihood of its successful implementation. Creating this sense of ownership starts with involving stakeholders in the change process from the beginning. By actively seeking their input and encouraging their participation in decision-making and planning, stakeholders are more likely to feel that they have a stake in the success of the change.

Communicating the benefits of the change in a way that resonates with stakeholders' personal and professional goals is also crucial. When stakeholders understand how the change aligns with their interests and contributes to their success, they are more likely to take an active role in ensuring its success. Transparency is key in building ownership and accountability. Keeping stakeholders informed about the progress of the change, the challenges encountered, and the strategies for addressing these challenges helps to build trust and reinforce their commitment to the initiative.

Setting clear expectations and roles is essential. Stakeholders should have a clear understanding of what is expected of them and how their contributions fit into the broader change effort. This clarity helps to prevent confusion and overlapping responsibilities, which can undermine ownership and accountability. Empowering stakeholders by giving them the autonomy to make decisions and take actions within their areas of responsibility encourages a sense of ownership. When stakeholders feel empowered, they are more likely to take initiative and be proactive in addressing challenges.

Recognizing and celebrating the contributions of stakeholders reinforces a sense of ownership and accountability. Acknowledging their efforts and achievements, both publicly and privately, can boost morale and motivate continued engagement and commitment. Regular feedback and open channels of communication allow stakeholders to voice their concerns, offer suggestions, and feel heard. This two-way communication fosters a collaborative environment where stakeholders feel valued and accountable.

Fostering a sense of ownership and accountability among stakeholders involves involving them in the change process, communicating benefits that resonate with their interests, maintaining transparency, setting clear expectations and roles, empowering stakeholders, recognizing their contributions, and ensuring regular feedback and open communication. These strategies help create an environment where stakeholders are motivated to actively contribute to and take responsibility for the success of the change initiative.

Empowering individuals to take transformative actions aligned with the change initiative is a crucial step in ensuring the effectiveness and sustainability of the change. This empowerment involves enabling and encouraging team members to not only support the change but to actively participate in driving it forward.

Central to this empowerment is providing individuals with the necessary tools, resources, and information to understand the change and its implications fully. When team members are well-informed, they can make better decisions and take actions that contribute positively to the change process. Training and development play a significant role in empowerment. Offering opportunities for skill enhancement and learning ensures that individuals are equipped to handle new challenges and responsibilities brought about by the change. This might include training sessions, workshops, or access to online learning resources.

Creating an environment where initiative and innovation are encouraged is also key. When individuals feel that their ideas are valued and that they have the freedom to experiment and take risks, they are more likely to take initiative and propose creative solutions. Leadership support is crucial in empowering individuals. Leaders who demonstrate trust in their team members' abilities and provide them with autonomy foster a sense of empowerment. Supportive leadership also means being available to provide guidance, answer questions, and offer feedback. Setting clear goals and expectations helps individuals understand what they need to achieve and how their actions contribute to the overall success of the change initiative. When goals are aligned with the change objectives, individuals can see the direct impact of their efforts on the organization's progress.

Recognizing and rewarding efforts and achievements is an effective way to empower individuals. Acknowledging contributions, whether through formal recognition programs or informal expressions of appreciation, reinforces the value of individual efforts and motivates continued engagement. Encouraging collaboration and peer support is another aspect of empowerment. When individuals work together, share knowledge, and support each other, it creates a collective sense of empowerment where everyone feels part of the change journey.

Empowering individuals to take transformative actions aligned with the change initiative involves providing necessary tools and information, offering training and development opportunities, encouraging initiative and innovation, supportive leadership, setting clear goals, recognizing and rewarding contributions, and fostering collaboration and peer support. These elements collectively create an environment where individuals are motivated and equipped to actively contribute to and drive the change initiative.

Chapter 5: Leading Transformation

Navigating the complexities of change leadership involves understanding and managing the multifaceted challenges that arise during the process of transforming an organization. This aspect of leadership is critical in guiding teams and the entire organization through the intricate journey of change. At the core of navigating these complexities is the ability to balance various elements of the organization – its people, processes, technology, and culture.

Leaders must understand how changes in one area can impact others, and they must be adept at aligning these components in a way that supports the overall objectives of the change initiative. Another key aspect is dealing with the uncertainty and ambiguity that often accompany change. Leaders need to be comfortable operating in environments where not all variables are known and where plans may need to be adjusted on the fly. This requires a combination of strategic foresight, adaptability, and resilience.

Effective change leaders also recognize the importance of managing the emotional journey of their teams. Change can elicit a range of emotions, from excitement and anticipation to fear and resistance. Leaders must be skilled in empathizing with these emotions, addressing concerns, and maintaining morale and motivation throughout the change process. Communication plays a pivotal role in navigating the complexities of change leadership. It's not just about disseminating information; it's about creating dialogue, fostering understanding, and building consensus. Leaders must be able to articulate the vision and the path forward in a way that is clear, compelling, and relatable.

Stakeholder management is another crucial element. Leaders must identify and engage with various stakeholders, understanding their perspectives, interests, and potential impact on the change process. Building and maintaining strong relationships with these stakeholders is key to ensuring support and minimizing resistance. Risk management is also a significant part of navigating change complexities. Leaders should anticipate potential risks and challenges and have strategies in place to mitigate them. This involves continuous monitoring and being prepared to make swift decisions to address issues as they arise. Navigating the complexities of change leadership requires a continuous learning mindset. Leaders must be open to feedback, willing to learn from both successes and failures, and continuously adapt their strategies and approaches.

Navigating the complexities of change leadership requires balancing multiple elements of the organization, managing uncertainty, addressing the emotional aspects of change, effective communication, stakeholder management, risk management, and a continuous learning mindset. Mastery of these aspects enables leaders to guide their organizations through the transformative journey of change successfully.

The intricate landscape of change leadership is a dynamic and multifaceted arena that requires leaders to navigate a variety of challenges and opportunities. At its core, this landscape is defined by the need to guide an organization through transformation while managing the complexities that such a process inevitably entails. Leaders encounter the challenge of aligning multiple facets of an organization with the change initiative. This involves synchronizing processes, technology, people, and culture, ensuring that each element not only adapts to the change but also contributes positively to it. The ability to see how these pieces fit together and to adjust them in harmony is crucial.

Leaders in this environment must also grapple with the inherent uncertainty and ambiguity of change. Change processes often involve venturing into uncharted territory, which requires a leader to be comfortable with not having all the answers and being able to make decisions in a landscape where factors and outcomes might not be fully predictable.

Managing the emotional journey of the workforce is another critical aspect of this landscape. Change can provoke a wide range of emotions among staff, from excitement and engagement to fear and resistance. A leader must navigate these emotional currents, providing support, understanding, and motivation to help team members navigate through these feelings. Effective communication is a cornerstone in the landscape of change leadership. It is the means by which leaders articulate the vision, share important updates, address concerns, and build a narrative that keeps everyone aligned and engaged with the change process.

Stakeholder management is also a vital component. Leaders must identify key stakeholders, understand their perspectives and concerns, and engage with them in a way that builds support and minimizes opposition. Each stakeholder group may have different needs and concerns, and addressing these effectively is key to maintaining momentum. Risk management is an integral part of navigating the landscape of change. Anticipating, identifying, and mitigating potential risks ensures that the change initiative remains on track and can adapt to challenges as they arise.

This landscape is one of continuous learning and adaptation. Leaders must be open to feedback, willing to adjust their strategies, and capable of learning from both successes and setbacks. This adaptability is essential in a landscape that is constantly evolving. The intricate landscape of change leadership is characterized by the need to align organizational elements, manage uncertainty, handle emotional dynamics, communicate effectively, manage stakeholders, address risks, and maintain a stance of continuous learning and adaptation. Navigating this landscape successfully is key to leading an organization through the transformative journey of change.

In leading transformation, one of the most critical tasks is to balance the technical aspects of change with the human side. This balance is essential to ensure that while the operational and strategic changes are efficiently managed, the emotional and psychological impact on the organization's people is also addressed with care and consideration.

The technical aspects of change typically involve the implementation of new systems, processes, or structures. Leaders must have a clear understanding of these elements and how they will enhance organizational performance. They need to ensure that the technical changes are feasible, well-planned, and aligned with the overall goals of the organization. This often requires a detailed approach, focusing on data, logistics, and measurable outcomes. However, focusing solely on the technical aspects can overlook the human element, which is crucial for the success of any change initiative. The human side of change addresses how the adjustments affect the employees, from their day-to-day tasks to their roles and responsibilities within the organization. It involves managing emotions, expectations, and reactions to the change.

Leaders must therefore also focus on the emotional journey of their teams. This includes understanding and addressing the concerns, fears, and resistance that might arise. Effective communication is key here, as it helps in explaining the reasons behind the change, its benefits, and how individuals and teams fit into the new structure. Empathy plays a significant role in balancing these two sides. Leaders need to empathize with the challenges that their teams face and provide support and encouragement. This might involve offering training and development opportunities to help team members acquire the necessary skills and feel more confident in their new roles.

Involving employees in the change process can also help balance the technical and human aspects. When employees are part of the planning and implementation phases, they are more likely to feel a sense of ownership and commitment to the change. This involvement can also provide valuable insights into potential issues or challenges from those who are directly affected by the change. Recognition and appreciation of efforts and achievements during the change process help in maintaining morale and motivation. Acknowledging the hard work and adaptability of teams can reinforce positive behavior and support a smoother transition.

Balancing the technical aspects of change with its human side involves a combination of strategic planning and empathetic leadership. This balance ensures that while operational goals are achieved, the people who make up the organization are also prepared, supported, and motivated to embrace and drive the change. Navigating the complexities of diverse stakeholder dynamics is a critical aspect of leading transformation. Successful change initiatives require understanding and managing the varied interests, perspectives, and influences of different stakeholder groups. These stakeholders can include employees, management, customers, suppliers, and even the wider community.

The first step in navigating these dynamics is to identify and understand the various stakeholders involved in the change. This involves recognizing their roles, expectations, and how the change will impact them. Each group may have different concerns and priorities, and understanding these nuances is key to addressing their needs effectively. Effective communication is essential in managing stakeholder dynamics. Leaders should develop tailored communication strategies for different stakeholder groups, ensuring that messages are relevant and resonate with each audience. Clear, consistent, and transparent communication helps in building trust and reducing misunderstandings or misinformation. Engaging stakeholders in the change process is also crucial. This can be achieved through forums, focus groups, or direct involvement in decision-making. When stakeholders feel they have a voice in the process, they are more likely to support and contribute positively to the change.

Managing expectations is another important aspect. Leaders should be realistic about what the change can and cannot achieve and communicate this clearly to avoid disappointment or resistance. Setting achievable goals and delivering on promises helps in building credibility and trust. Conflict resolution skills are important in navigating stakeholder dynamics. Differences in opinions and interests can lead to conflicts, and leaders must be equipped to handle these situations constructively. This involves listening to all parties, understanding the root cause of the conflict, and finding mutually acceptable solutions.

Building and maintaining relationships is key to effective stakeholder management. Regular interactions, showing appreciation for stakeholder input, and being responsive to their concerns can strengthen these relationships. Strong relationships can be invaluable, especially when navigating difficult aspects of the change process. Flexibility and adaptability are also important. Stakeholder dynamics can change as the change initiative progresses, and leaders need to be able to adapt their strategies accordingly. Being open to feedback and willing to make adjustments demonstrates a commitment to the stakeholders' interests.

Navigating the complexities of diverse stakeholder dynamics involves understanding stakeholder perspectives, effective and tailored communication, stakeholder engagement, managing expectations, conflict resolution, relationship building, and flexibility. Successfully managing these dynamics is crucial for gaining support and ensuring the successful implementation of change initiatives. Recognizing and mitigating common pitfalls in change processes is an essential skill for leaders driving transformation. Change initiatives, despite being well-planned, often encounter obstacles that can hinder progress. Being aware of these potential pitfalls and having strategies to address them can significantly increase the chances of successful change implementation.

One common pitfall is resistance to change. This resistance often stems from fear of the unknown, comfort with the status quo, or a perceived threat to one's role or status. To mitigate this, leaders should focus on clear and empathetic communication, actively involve employees in the change process, and provide adequate support and training. Another pitfall is inadequate communication. The failure to communicate the vision, benefits, and progress of the change effectively can lead to misinformation, rumors, and increased resistance. Leaders should ensure regular, transparent, and two-way communication to keep everyone informed and engaged.

Lack of stakeholder engagement is also a frequent obstacle. Without the active support and involvement of key stakeholders, change initiatives can lose momentum and direction. Leaders should identify and involve all relevant stakeholders from the outset, understanding their concerns and motivations. Underestimating the resources required for the change is another common issue. This includes time, budget, and human resources. Adequate planning and allocation of resources are necessary to ensure that the change initiative has the support it needs to succeed.

Failing to align the change with the organization's culture can also derail the process. If the change is perceived as being at odds with the organization's values and norms, it will face greater resistance. Leaders should strive to align the change with the organization's culture or work to evolve the culture in line with the change. Neglecting the need for quick wins is a pitfall that can affect morale and momentum. Demonstrating early successes, even small ones, can build confidence and support for the change initiative. Leaders should identify opportunities for early victories and communicate these to the organization.

Ignoring the emotional impact of change on employees can lead to decreased morale and engagement. Leaders should acknowledge and address the emotional aspects, providing support where needed and recognizing the efforts of those involved in the change. Overlooking the need for continuous monitoring and adaptation can lead to the change initiative going off course. Regularly reviewing progress, seeking feedback, and being willing to make adjustments are crucial for the long-term success of the change.

Recognizing and mitigating common pitfalls in change processes involves addressing resistance to change, ensuring adequate communication, engaging stakeholders, allocating sufficient resources, aligning the change with organizational culture, achieving quick wins, managing the emotional impact, and continuously monitoring and adapting the change process. By being aware of and proactively managing these pitfalls, leaders can navigate the complexities of change more effectively.

In change initiatives, recognizing common challenges and pitfalls is vital for leaders to effectively navigate the transformation process. A deep understanding of these potential issues enables leaders to proactively develop strategies to mitigate them, enhancing the chances of a successful outcome. Resistance to change is perhaps the most frequent challenge. It can manifest due to various reasons, including fear of the unknown, discomfort with new processes, or perceived threats to job security. Identifying this resistance early and understanding its root causes is essential for addressing it effectively. Inadequate communication often leads to misunderstandings about the goals and benefits of the change, resulting in confusion or lack of buy-in. Ensuring that communication is clear, consistent, and reaches all levels of the organization is crucial for keeping everyone aligned and engaged. Another common pitfall is failing to secure sufficient stakeholder buy-in. Change initiatives can falter without the active support of key individuals or groups, including senior leadership, middle management, or frontline employees. Identifying and engaging these stakeholders from the outset is crucial.

Underestimating the resource requirements, whether in terms of time, budget, or personnel, can lead to unrealistic expectations and strain on the organization. Accurate assessment and allocation of resources are necessary for the smooth execution of the change process. Neglecting the alignment of the change initiative with the organization's culture can cause friction and resistance. Leaders must ensure that the change is compatible with or thoughtfully integrated into the organization's existing cultural fabric. Overlooking the need for quick wins can affect the momentum and morale of the change initiative. Identifying and celebrating early successes helps build confidence and demonstrates the benefits of the change. Another challenge is managing the emotional impact of change. Change can be unsettling for employees, and not addressing the emotional aspect can lead to disengagement or attrition. Leaders need to be empathetic and supportive in their approach.

Failing to adapt and adjust the change strategy when faced with new information or challenges can result in the initiative becoming irrelevant or ineffective. Continuous monitoring and flexibility are key to ensuring the change remains on track and achieves its objectives.

Identifying common challenges and pitfalls in change initiatives involves recognizing and addressing resistance to change, ensuring effective communication, securing stakeholder buy-in, accurately assessing resource needs, aligning the change with organizational culture, achieving quick wins, managing the emotional impact, and remaining flexible and adaptable. Awareness and proactive management of these issues are critical for the successful navigation of change.

Learning from real-world examples of setbacks in change processes is invaluable. These examples provide powerful lessons that can inform future strategies and help avoid similar pitfalls. Analyzing cases where change initiatives did not go as planned offers insights into the complexities of managing change and highlights the importance of adaptability and resilience. One key learning from such examples is the critical role of clear and consistent communication. Many change initiatives falter when the reasons for change are not effectively communicated to all stakeholders, leading to confusion and resistance. Understanding the nuances of how successful communication strategies were not implemented can guide future efforts.

Another lesson is the significance of stakeholder engagement. Setbacks often occur when key stakeholders are not adequately involved in the change process. Analyzing these scenarios can shed light on the importance of understanding stakeholder needs and involving them actively in planning and implementation. Resource allocation is another area where many change processes encounter difficulties. Real-world setbacks demonstrate the consequences of underestimating the resources required for change, including time, finances, and human capital. Learning from these instances emphasizes the need for thorough planning and realistic budgeting.

Many setbacks are linked to a failure to align the change initiative with the organization's culture. These examples highlight the challenges of introducing changes that do not resonate with the existing values and practices of the organization, underlining the need for cultural considerations in change planning. Resistance to change is a common theme in many setbacks. Studying these cases reveals various factors that contribute to resistance, including fear of the unknown, perceived threats to job security, and discomfort with new ways of working. Lessons from these examples stress the importance of managing resistance through empathy, support, and effective change management strategies.

Leadership plays a pivotal role in the success or failure of change initiatives. Setbacks often occur when leaders are not fully committed or lack the skills to guide the change process. Analyzing these situations can provide insights into the qualities and actions of effective change leaders. Flexibility and adaptability are crucial in managing change, as evidenced by setbacks in rigidly managed initiatives. Learning from these examples highlights the importance of being responsive to feedback, willing to make adjustments, and capable of navigating unforeseen challenges.

Learning from real-world examples of setbacks in change processes provides valuable lessons in effective communication, stakeholder engagement, resource allocation, cultural alignment, resistance management, leadership, and the need for flexibility. These insights are instrumental in shaping more robust and resilient strategies for future change initiatives. Maintaining momentum in change initiatives is crucial for their success and sustainability. Leveraging various instruments and tools can significantly aid in keeping the momentum going, ensuring that the change process remains dynamic and on track.

Performance tracking tools are vital in monitoring the progress of the change initiative. Tools like dashboards and project management software allow leaders and teams to keep a close eye on key milestones, deliverables, and deadlines. They provide real-time insights into the progress of the change, helping to identify areas where the initiative is on track and areas that require more attention. Communication platforms play a continuous role in maintaining change momentum. Regular updates, success stories, and transparent discussions about challenges keep the change initiative visible and top of mind for everyone involved. These platforms ensure that all stakeholders stay informed and engaged throughout the process.

Feedback mechanisms are essential for gauging the effectiveness of the change and the level of stakeholder engagement. Surveys, feedback forms, and suggestion boxes allow stakeholders to voice their opinions, concerns, and suggestions, providing valuable input that can help refine and improve the change process. Training and development tools remain crucial throughout the change process. As the change progresses, new skills or knowledge might be required. E-learning platforms, workshops, and training sessions ensure that all individuals have the necessary competencies to support and sustain the change.

Collaboration tools facilitate ongoing teamwork and problem-solving. Tools that support virtual meetings, shared workspaces, and collaborative document editing enable teams to work together effectively, even if they are geographically dispersed. Recognition and reward systems help in maintaining morale and motivation. Acknowledging individual and team contributions to the change initiative reinforces positive behaviors and encourages continued involvement and support.

Change management software can offer structured frameworks for managing various aspects of the change process. These tools can assist in risk management, stakeholder mapping, and change impact analysis, providing a comprehensive approach to maintaining change momentum. Analytics tools continue to be important for making data-driven decisions. They can provide insights into the impact of the change on various aspects of the organization, helping leaders to make informed decisions about the future course of the initiative.

Leveraging instruments and tools to maintain change momentum involves using performance tracking tools, communication platforms, feedback mechanisms, training and development tools, collaboration tools, recognition and reward systems, change management software, and analytics tools. These resources help keep the change process focused, dynamic, and aligned with its objectives, ensuring ongoing engagement and success.

Utilizing the right instruments and tools is crucial for sustaining momentum in change initiatives. These resources play a key role in keeping the change process active, engaging, and aligned with its objectives. Change Management Dashboards are powerful tools for maintaining visibility of the change process. They provide a snapshot of key metrics and progress indicators, helping leaders and teams stay informed about the status of various change activities and milestones. Engagement Platforms facilitate continuous communication and interaction among stakeholders. Regular updates, discussion forums, and Q&A sessions hosted on these platforms help keep the conversation about the change alive and foster a sense of community around the change initiative.

Feedback and Survey Tools are essential for capturing the pulse of the organization. Regular surveys and feedback channels provide insights into how the change is being perceived and experienced at different levels, allowing for timely adjustments to strategies and approaches. Learning and Development Tools are important for reinforcing new skills and behaviors. Continuous access to training resources, e-learning modules, and skill-building programs ensures that employees remain equipped and confident to handle the evolving demands of the change process.

Collaborative Workspaces, both physical and digital, encourage teamwork and collective problem-solving. These spaces are critical for brainstorming, innovation, and cross-functional collaboration, all of which contribute to maintaining momentum. Recognition and Incentive Programs help sustain enthusiasm and motivation. Celebrating milestones, acknowledging individual and team contributions, and providing incentives for desired behaviors reinforce the value of the change and encourage ongoing participation.

Analytical Tools play a significant role in measuring the impact of the change. Data gathered from various sources can be analyzed to understand the effectiveness of the change initiatives, identify areas for improvement, and inform future actions. Mobile Applications and Notifications can be used to provide timely updates and reminders. Push notifications and mobile access to change-related information ensure that stakeholders remain connected and engaged, even on the go. Social Media and Internal Blogs can be leveraged to share success stories, best practices, and testimonials related to the change. These platforms can generate a buzz around the change and help in creating a positive narrative. Risk Management Tools remain important throughout the change process. Continuously identifying, assessing, and mitigating risks ensures that the change initiative stays on course and is resilient to potential disruptions.

Sustaining change momentum involves utilizing a variety of tools and instruments, including change management dashboards, engagement platforms, feedback tools, learning and development resources, collaborative workspaces, recognition programs, analytical tools, mobile applications, social media, and risk management tools. These resources help keep stakeholders engaged, informed, and equipped to drive and support the change initiative. Reinforcing positive change behaviors and practices is a critical element in sustaining momentum and ensuring the long-term success of change initiatives. It involves encouraging and solidifying the behaviors and activities that align with the change objectives, making them a natural and integral part of the organization's culture.

One effective way to reinforce positive behaviors is through recognition and rewards. Acknowledging and rewarding individuals and teams who demonstrate the desired behaviors and practices not only motivates them to continue these actions but also sets an example for others. This can be done through formal recognition programs, informal acknowledgments, or performance-based incentives. Consistent communication plays a pivotal role in reinforcement. Regularly highlighting the importance of the change behaviors, sharing success stories, and demonstrating the impact of these behaviors on the organization's goals keeps them at the forefront of everyone's mind. This consistent messaging reinforces the value and importance of the new behaviors. Providing ongoing training and development opportunities is also key. As the organization evolves, ensuring that employees have the skills and knowledge to adapt to new processes and systems is crucial. Continuous learning environments encourage the adoption of new behaviors and support their integration into daily work.

Leadership modeling is another powerful tool for reinforcement. When leaders exemplify the behaviors and practices that the change initiative seeks to promote, it sends a strong message about their importance. Leaders should consistently demonstrate these behaviors in their actions and decisions. Creating a supportive environment that encourages the new behaviors is essential. This includes providing the necessary resources and tools, creating policies and procedures that align with the change, and fostering a culture that values innovation, flexibility, and continuous improvement.

Feedback loops are important for reinforcing positive change behaviors. Regular feedback allows individuals to understand how their actions align with the change objectives and where adjustments might be needed. Constructive feedback helps in fine-tuning behaviors and practices for better alignment with the change goals. Celebrating milestones and successes associated with the change behaviors helps in maintaining enthusiasm and commitment. Marking these achievements, big or small, reinforces the progress being made and the collective effort towards the change.

Reinforcing positive change behaviors and practices involves recognition and rewards, consistent communication, ongoing training and development, leadership modeling, creating a supportive environment, establishing feedback loops, and celebrating milestones and successes. These strategies are crucial in making the desired behaviors a lasting part of the organization's culture, thereby ensuring the success and sustainability of the change initiative.

In the context of leading transformation, the ability to adapt and evolve tools to meet the changing needs of the organization is crucial. As change initiatives progress, the needs and challenges of the organization can shift, requiring tools and approaches to be flexible and responsive. Adapting tools to meet evolving needs involves regularly reviewing and assessing the effectiveness of the current tools being used. This assessment can be based on feedback from users, performance metrics, and the overall progress of the change initiative. Understanding how well these tools are supporting the change objectives is key to determining if adjustments or replacements are necessary.

Technological advancements and emerging trends should be monitored continuously. The rapid pace of technological change means that new and more effective tools are constantly being developed. Staying abreast of these developments can provide opportunities to incorporate more efficient or user-friendly tools into the change process. Customization of tools to fit the specific context of the organization is often necessary. Off-the-shelf solutions might not always align perfectly with the organization's unique needs. Customizing these tools, or developing bespoke solutions, ensures that they are more closely aligned with the specific requirements of the change initiative.

Training and support systems should evolve alongside the tools. As new tools are introduced or existing ones are modified, ensuring that employees have the necessary training to use these tools effectively is crucial. This might involve creating new training modules, updating resource materials, or offering additional support channels. Feedback loops are essential in adapting tools. Regular feedback from the users of these tools provides insights into how they could be improved or adapted. Encouraging open and honest feedback and acting on it demonstrates a commitment to continuously improving the change process.

Scalability and integration are important considerations. Tools should be scalable to accommodate the growth and expansion of the organization or the change initiative. They should also be able to integrate seamlessly with other systems and tools used in the organization to ensure a cohesive approach. Iterative development and implementation of tools allow for gradual improvement and adaptation. Rather than making large, sweeping changes to tools, an iterative approach enables small, manageable modifications to be made over time, reducing disruption and allowing for continuous improvement.

Adapting and evolving tools to meet evolving change needs involves regular assessment and review, staying updated on technological advancements, customization, evolving training and support, establishing feedback loops, considering scalability and integration, and adopting an iterative approach to development and implementation. These strategies ensure that the tools used in the change process remain effective, relevant, and supportive of the organization's evolving needs.

Effectively communicating change messages is a critical aspect of leading transformation. It involves conveying information about the change in a manner that is clear, persuasive, and resonates with the audience. Effective communication not only informs but also engages and motivates stakeholders, helping to build support for the change.

Clarity is paramount in change communication. Messages should be concise, specific, and easily understandable. Avoiding jargon and technical language ensures that the message is accessible to all members of the organization, regardless of their role or level. Consistency in messaging reinforces the change objectives and helps to build trust. Disparate or conflicting messages can lead to confusion and skepticism. Consistent messages, delivered through various channels and from different leaders, strengthen the credibility of the change initiative.

Tailoring messages to different audiences is crucial. Different stakeholder groups may have different concerns, priorities, and levels of understanding about the change. Customizing the message to address the specific needs and perspectives of each group ensures that it is more relevant and impactful. Using a variety of communication channels helps to reach a wider audience and cater to different preferences. This might include emails, meetings, social media, internal newsletters, and face-to-face interactions. A multi-channel approach ensures that the message is more likely to be received and absorbed.

Storytelling and the use of real-life examples can make change messages more engaging and memorable. Sharing stories of success, challenges overcome, or the potential impact of the change can help to illustrate the benefits and bring the message to life. Transparency is essential in change communication. Being open about the reasons for the change, the expected outcomes, and the challenges helps to build trust and respect. Acknowledging uncertainty and being honest about what is known and what is still to be determined can prevent misinformation and rumors.

Two-way communication is important for engagement. Providing opportunities for feedback, questions, and dialogue allows stakeholders to feel heard and valued. This can be facilitated through Q&A sessions, feedback forms, town hall meetings, or interactive workshops. Regular updates keep the momentum of the change initiative and maintain stakeholder engagement. Providing ongoing information about the progress, celebrating milestones, and discussing next steps keeps the change initiative visible and top of mind.

Effectively communicating change messages involves clarity, consistency, audience-specific messaging, using multiple channels, storytelling, transparency, two-way communication, and regular updates. These elements are crucial in ensuring that change messages are not only heard but also understood, accepted, and supported by all stakeholders. The art of crafting and delivering impactful change messages lies at the heart of effective change management. It is about creating a narrative that resonates with the audience, inspires action, and fosters a positive attitude towards the change. This process involves both the content of the message and the manner in which it is communicated.

Crafting impactful messages starts with a deep understanding of the change's purpose and benefits. The message should clearly articulate why the change is necessary and how it aligns with the organization's broader goals and values. It should convey a vision of the future that is compelling and desirable. The language used in crafting these messages is crucial. It should be simple, clear, and jargon-free, making the message accessible to everyone in the organization. The tone should be positive and inclusive, emphasizing opportunities and benefits rather than dwelling on challenges and risks.

Empathy is a key component in crafting change messages. Understanding the concerns and perspectives of the audience allows for a message that acknowledges these feelings and addresses them directly. This empathy helps in building trust and reducing resistance. As we mentioned before, storytelling can be a powerful tool in delivering change messages. Stories of success, examples of positive outcomes, or narratives that people can relate to can make the change more tangible and engaging. Stories help in illustrating the practical implications of the change and can be more persuasive than abstract descriptions.

The timing and context of delivering the message are also important. Messages should be delivered at a time when they are most relevant and in a context that makes sense to the audience. This could mean aligning the message with key organizational events or milestones. Choosing the right medium for delivering the message is essential. Different audiences may prefer different communication channels, such as email, social media, face-to-face meetings, or internal broadcasts. Using a variety of channels ensures a wider reach and higher impact.

Engaging and interactive communication can enhance the effectiveness of change messages. Encouraging dialogue, inviting questions, and seeking feedback make the communication process more dynamic and participatory. Consistency in messaging is crucial. Repeating key themes and messages helps reinforce the change narrative and ensures that it is remembered and understood. However, this repetition should be balanced to avoid message fatigue.

The art of crafting and delivering impactful change messages involves understanding the purpose of the change, using clear and empathetic language, storytelling, considering timing and context, choosing appropriate communication mediums, engaging in interactive communication, and maintaining consistency. These elements collectively contribute to creating change messages that are not only heard but resonate deeply with the audience, motivating them to embrace and participate in the change process. Engaging and inspiring stakeholders through effective communication is a fundamental aspect of successful change management. It's about creating a connection with stakeholders that goes beyond mere information sharing – it involves motivating them, winning their support, and encouraging their active participation in the change process.

To engage stakeholders effectively, it's crucial to understand their perspectives, concerns, and interests. This understanding allows for the creation of messages that are relevant and meaningful to different groups. Knowing what matters to each stakeholder group helps in crafting a narrative that resonates with their specific motivations and concerns. Personalizing communication is key to engagement. While broad messages are important for consistency, tailoring communication to address the unique questions and needs of different stakeholder groups makes the communication more relevant and impactful. This might involve segmenting the audience and developing targeted messages for each segment Interactive communication methods can significantly boost engagement. Instead of one-way communication, interactive methods like workshops, town halls, and discussion forums encourage dialogue and allow stakeholders to voice their opinions and concerns. This two-way communication fosters a sense of involvement and investment in the change process.

Transparency is essential for building trust and credibility. Openly sharing information about the change process, including challenges and how they are being addressed, builds stakeholder confidence. Transparency shows that the leadership is committed to honesty and integrity, which are crucial for winning stakeholder trust. Consistent and regular communication maintains engagement. Providing ongoing updates about the progress of the change, next steps, and celebrating milestones keeps stakeholders informed and involved. Regular communication helps to sustain interest and momentum in the change initiative.

Visual and multimedia elements can enhance the appeal and clarity of the communication. Using infographics, videos, and presentations can make complex information more understandable and engaging. These elements can break down barriers to understanding and add an engaging layer to the communication. Recognition of stakeholder contributions reinforces engagement. Acknowledging the input and efforts of stakeholders, whether through formal recognition programs or informal appreciation, shows that their contributions are valued and important.

Engaging and inspiring stakeholders through effective communication involves understanding their perspectives, personalizing communication, using interactive methods, maintaining transparency, ensuring consistent communication, utilizing visual and multimedia elements, and recognizing contributions. These strategies help build a strong connection with stakeholders, encouraging their enthusiastic support and active participation in the change initiative.

Maintaining transparency and openness throughout the transformation process is critical for building trust, managing expectations, and fostering a culture of inclusivity. Transparency in change management encourages stakeholder buy-in and helps to mitigate resistance by ensuring that everyone understands the what, why, and how of the change.

1. Open Communication Channels: Establish and maintain open lines of communication throughout the organization. This includes regular updates, open-door policies, and forums where employees can ask questions and express concerns. Ensuring that communication flows in both directions – from leadership to employees and vice versa – is essential for maintaining transparency.

2. Regular Updates: Provide regular updates on the progress of the transformation, including achievements, challenges faced, and the steps being taken to address them. This could be in the form of newsletters, email bulletins, or regular meetings. Transparency about both successes and setbacks keeps everyone informed and engaged.

3. Honesty in Communication: Be honest in all communications regarding the change. This means openly discussing the challenges and potential downsides, not just the benefits. Honesty builds trust and shows respect for the intelligence and maturity of all stakeholders.

4. Involving Stakeholders: Actively involve stakeholders in the change process. This can include surveys to gather input, collaborative planning sessions, and feedback mechanisms. When stakeholders feel that their opinions are valued and considered, it enhances transparency and builds a sense of ownership.

5. Feedback Mechanisms: Implement effective feedback mechanisms to gather responses and reactions to the change process. This could include suggestion boxes, feedback forms, or focus groups. Actively reviewing and responding to feedback demonstrates a commitment to openness.

6. Cultural Shifts: Work towards embedding transparency and openness into the organization's culture. This involves modeling these behaviors at the leadership level and recognizing and rewarding transparency in others. Creating a culture where openness is valued is key to sustaining it.

7. Training on Transparency: Provide training and resources to managers and team leaders on how to communicate transparently and effectively. Equip them with the skills to handle difficult conversations, share sensitive information, and engage in active listening.

8. Celebrating Transparency: Recognize and celebrate instances where transparency led to positive outcomes. Sharing these success stories can encourage others to practice transparency and reinforce its value in the organization.

9. Documenting the Process: Keep detailed records of the transformation process, including decisions made, actions taken, and the rationale behind them. This documentation can provide clarity and serve as a valuable resource for understanding the journey of the change.

Maintaining transparency and openness throughout the transformation process involves open communication channels, regular updates, honesty, stakeholder involvement, effective feedback mechanisms, cultural shifts towards openness, training on transparent communication, celebrating transparency, and thorough documentation. These strategies collectively foster an environment of trust and collaboration, which is essential for the success of any transformation initiative.

Chapter 6: Sustaining the Momentum

Maintaining continued momentum in change initiatives is vital for their success. Momentum keeps the energy and drive of the change initiative alive, ensuring that the transformation process moves forward and achieves its goals. When momentum is sustained, it helps to overcome resistance, prevents stagnation, and builds a sense of progress and achievement among all involved. The sustained momentum ensures that the change initiative remains a priority within the organization. It prevents the initiative from being overshadowed by other daily operations or new projects, keeping the focus on achieving the change objectives. This focus is crucial for ensuring that the resources, both time and financial, are continuously allocated to the change effort.

When momentum is maintained, it also helps in embedding the change into the organizational culture. Continuous effort and focus make the new ways of working more familiar and habitual, increasing the likelihood of the change being successfully integrated into the organization's standard practices. Sustained momentum helps in building and maintaining stakeholder engagement. When stakeholders see continuous progress and commitment to the change initiative, their belief in and support for the change is reinforced. This ongoing engagement is critical for the overall success of the change.

The continued momentum also provides opportunities for learning and improvement. As the change initiative progresses, continuous effort allows for the gathering of insights and feedback, which can be used to refine and improve the change process. This learning is essential for the long-term sustainability and effectiveness of the change. Additionally, sustaining momentum is important for morale and motivation. Regular progress and achievements provide positive reinforcement for those involved in the change initiative. This reinforcement boosts morale and motivation, encouraging continued effort and support for the change.

1. Continuous Communication: Keep the lines of communication open and active. Regular updates about the progress of the change initiative, upcoming steps, and any modifications to the plan help keep everyone aligned and informed. This continuous flow of information helps prevent rumors and misinformation, which can derail momentum.

2. Visible Leadership Commitment: Leaders should continue to demonstrate their commitment to the change. This can be achieved through their active involvement in change-related activities, consistent messaging about the importance of the change, and visibly modeling the behaviors and practices that the change is promoting.

3. Reinforcing the Vision and Goals: Regularly reiterating the vision and goals of the change initiative helps remind everyone of the 'big picture' and why the change is important. This reinforcement can be integrated into regular meetings, internal communications, and performance objectives.

4. Celebrating Milestones and Successes: Recognizing and celebrating key milestones and successes, no matter how small, can boost morale and motivate continued effort towards the change. Celebrations and acknowledgments serve as positive reinforcement and help maintain enthusiasm.

5. Addressing Challenges Proactively: Stay vigilant to new challenges and obstacles that may emerge. Addressing these proactively and transparently ensures that they don't become roadblocks to progress. Encouraging a culture of problem-solving and resilience helps sustain momentum.

6. Empowering Change Champions: Identify and empower change champions within the organization – individuals who are enthusiastic and influential about the change. These

champions can act as advocates, helping to spread positive messages and encourage their peers to embrace the change.

7. Ongoing Training and Support: As the change becomes more embedded, continue to provide training and support to staff. This ensures that everyone has the skills and knowledge they need to work effectively in the new environment and helps to mitigate any performance dips related to the change.

8. Monitoring and Feedback: Implement mechanisms for regular monitoring of the change progress and for gathering feedback. Use this data to make informed adjustments to the change strategy, ensuring that it remains relevant and effective.

9. Building on the Change: Look for opportunities to build on the initial change, leveraging its successes for further improvement and innovation. This approach can help maintain a dynamic and continuous improvement environment.

In change initiatives, implementing strategies to prevent stagnation and regression is essential for maintaining momentum and ensuring continuous progress. Stagnation can occur when the initial excitement of the change wanes, and regression can happen when there's a tendency to revert to old habits and practices. One effective strategy is to set and communicate short-term goals alongside the long-term objectives of the change initiative. These smaller, achievable goals provide ongoing targets and milestones, keeping the team focused and creating a sense of continuous achievement and progress. Regularly reviewing and adjusting the change strategy based on current circumstances and feedback is crucial. This approach allows for the flexibility to address emerging challenges and adapt to changing conditions, preventing stagnation by keeping the strategy relevant and effective.

Creating a culture of continuous improvement where feedback is encouraged and acted upon can also prevent stagnation. In such a culture, employees are motivated to look for ways to improve processes and practices continuously, contributing to the forward momentum of the change initiative. Empowering employees to take ownership of parts of the change process is another important strategy. When team members feel a sense of responsibility and autonomy, they are more likely to take initiative and drive progress, thereby preventing regression to old ways of working.

Regular communication about the benefits and successes of the change helps maintain enthusiasm and commitment. Highlighting how the changes are positively impacting the organization and individuals helps to reinforce the value of the new approaches and practices. Providing ongoing training and development ensures that employees have the skills and knowledge required to adapt to the new ways of working. This ongoing investment in staff development helps to prevent regression by equipping employees with the tools they need to succeed in the changed environment.

Recognizing and rewarding efforts and achievements related to the change initiative can also prevent stagnation. Acknowledgment and appreciation of the hard work and adaptability of employees reinforce positive behaviors and encourage continued commitment to the change. Fostering a supportive environment where challenges and difficulties can be openly discussed and addressed is key to preventing regression. This supportive atmosphere ensures that employees feel comfortable seeking help and are less likely to revert to familiar but outdated practices when faced with challenges.

Preventing stagnation and regression in change initiatives involves setting and communicating short-term goals, regularly reviewing and adjusting the strategy, fostering a culture of continuous improvement, empowering employees, regularly communicating about benefits and successes, providing ongoing training, recognizing and rewarding efforts, and fostering a supportive environment. Maintaining enthusiasm and engagement among stakeholders is essential for the ongoing success of change initiatives. Stakeholder enthusiasm fuels the momentum of the change process, while their engagement ensures that the change is supported and embraced across the organization.

Regular and transparent communication is key to maintaining stakeholder enthusiasm and engagement. Keeping stakeholders informed about the progress of the change, upcoming steps, and how their input is influencing the change process helps them feel connected and valued. This communication should not just focus on successes but also openly address challenges and how they are being managed. Involving stakeholders in the change process fosters a deeper sense of engagement. When stakeholders have opportunities to contribute their ideas and feedback, they are more likely to feel a sense of ownership and commitment to the change. This involvement can range from decision-making roles to participation in feedback sessions or change implementation teams.

Recognizing and celebrating milestones, even small ones, helps maintain enthusiasm. Acknowledging the hard work and achievements of those involved in the change process reinforces their efforts and motivates continued progress. Celebrations and recognition can take various forms, from formal award ceremonies to informal team acknowledgments. Providing ongoing support and resources is crucial in maintaining engagement. Stakeholders may need additional training, tools, or information to adapt to the change effectively. Ensuring that these needs are met demonstrates the organization's commitment to supporting its people through the change.

Creating a positive narrative around the change can also sustain enthusiasm. This narrative should highlight the benefits of the change, success stories, and how the change aligns with the organization's values and vision. A compelling and positive story can be a powerful motivator. Fostering a culture of collaboration and inclusivity enhances stakeholder engagement. Encouraging open dialogue, cross-functional teamwork, and a sense of community around the change initiative makes stakeholders feel they are part of something significant and positive.

Leadership plays a crucial role in maintaining enthusiasm and engagement. Leaders who are visibly committed to the change, who communicate effectively, and who demonstrate empathy and support for their teams can inspire and motivate stakeholders throughout the change process. Continuously gauging stakeholder sentiment through surveys, feedback mechanisms, and direct conversations allows for adjustments to be made to keep stakeholders engaged. Understanding their concerns, challenges, and perceptions of the change helps in making timely and relevant adjustments to the change strategy.

Maintaining enthusiasm and engagement among stakeholders in change initiatives involves regular and transparent communication, involving stakeholders in the process, recognizing and celebrating milestones, providing ongoing support, creating a positive narrative, fostering a collaborative and inclusive culture, visible and effective leadership, and continuously gauging stakeholder sentiment.

Overcoming setbacks and challenges is an integral part of sustaining the momentum in change initiatives. Setbacks are inevitable in any transformation process, but how they are handled can significantly impact the success and resilience of the change.

1. Anticipating and Planning for Setbacks: Proactive identification of potential challenges and planning for them can mitigate their impact. This involves risk assessment and contingency planning. By anticipating possible hurdles, leaders can prepare strategies to address them effectively, reducing the likelihood of being caught off guard.

2. Open and Honest Communication: When setbacks occur, transparent communication is crucial. Informing stakeholders about the nature of the setback, its implications, and the steps being taken to address it fosters trust and keeps everyone aligned. It's important to maintain a balance between being honest about the challenges and maintaining a positive outlook.

3. Learning from Setbacks: Each challenge presents an opportunity to learn and grow. Analyzing why the setback occurred and what can be learned from it helps in refining

strategies and processes. This learning mindset turns challenges into valuable experiences that strengthen the change initiative.

4. Flexibility and Adaptability: Being flexible and adaptable in the face of challenges is key. Sometimes, setbacks may require changes to the original plan or approach. Being willing to make these adjustments and adapt strategies based on new information or changing circumstances keeps the initiative dynamic and responsive.

5. Engaging Stakeholders in Problem-Solving: Involving stakeholders in addressing setbacks can be empowering and can generate innovative solutions. Collective problem-solving not only harnesses diverse perspectives but also reinforces stakeholder commitment to the change process.

6. Maintaining Positivity and Resilience: Keeping a positive attitude and demonstrating resilience in the face of setbacks inspires the same qualities in others. Leaders should model a positive approach to overcoming challenges, emphasizing the long-term vision and the overall benefits of the change.

7. Reinforcing the Vision and Goals: Reminding stakeholders of the ultimate goals and vision of the change helps to put setbacks into perspective. It reinforces the importance of the change and why persevering through challenges is worthwhile.

8. Providing Support and Resources: Ensuring that teams have the support and resources they need to overcome challenges is important. This might include additional training, access to expert advice, or allocating more time or resources to certain areas of the change initiative.

In sustaining the momentum of change initiatives, it's crucial to identify common setbacks and challenges that can impede long-term sustainability. Understanding these potential issues helps in developing strategies to address them proactively. Resistance to change often persists or resurfaces, especially if stakeholders do not see immediate benefits or if the change process is prolonged. This resistance can manifest as skepticism, decreased productivity, or overt opposition to the new ways of working. Loss of focus and priority can occur as the initial enthusiasm wanes or other organizational priorities emerge. This can lead to the change initiative being sidelined or deprioritized, hindering its progress and implementation.

Resource constraints, such as budget cuts, staff turnover, or competing projects, can impact the ability to sustain change. Limited resources can slow down or halt the progress of change initiatives, leading to frustration and skepticism among stakeholders. Fatigue and burnout among team members and leaders can set in, especially in long and demanding change processes. This can lead to decreased engagement, lower energy levels, and a decline in the overall momentum of the change initiative. Inadequate communication and follow-up can lead to misunderstandings, misinformation, or a lack of clarity about the current status and future direction of the change. This can result in stakeholders feeling disconnected from the process. Failure to embed change into the organizational culture can threaten the sustainability of the change. If the new behaviors, processes, or systems are not fully integrated into the day-to-day operations and values of the organization, there is a risk of reverting to old ways.

Lack of visible leadership support and reinforcement of change can lead to a decline in stakeholder commitment and engagement. Continuous leadership support is essential for maintaining momentum and reinforcing the importance of the change. Difficulty in measuring and demonstrating the impact of the change can lead to questions about its value and effectiveness. Without clear metrics and tangible results, it can be challenging to maintain support and enthusiasm for the initiative.

Building resilience and adaptability in the face of obstacles is a key factor in maintaining the momentum of change initiatives. This involves nurturing a mindset that views challenges as opportunities for learning and growth, transforming how obstacles are perceived and approached. Creating a supportive organizational culture is essential, where risk-taking is encouraged, and learning from failures is seen as part of the journey. This kind of environment fosters innovation and experimentation, crucial for adaptability. Flexibility in planning and execution allows teams to modify their approaches in response to new information or unexpected challenges, keeping strategies relevant and effective.

Equipping teams with the necessary skills to adapt to changing circumstances is also vital. Training in problem-solving, critical thinking, and change management enhances their capacity to deal with challenges effectively. Open communication and feedback are crucial in this process, as they enable early identification of issues and collaborative problem-solving. Engaging in scenario planning helps anticipate potential challenges and develop strategies to address them. This proactive approach prepares the organization for various eventualities, reducing the impact of obstacles when they arise. Additionally, encouraging the building of strong support networks, both within and outside the organization, can provide diverse perspectives and solutions.

Acknowledging the importance of physical and mental well-being in building resilience is also key. Practices that support well-being, such as maintaining a work-life balance and stress management techniques, are crucial for sustaining momentum. Celebrating instances where teams successfully navigate challenges reinforces the value of resilience and adaptability, motivating continued effort. Implementing a process for reviewing setbacks to extract lessons learned is critical. Understanding what went wrong and how it was addressed refines strategies and helps avoid similar issues in the future, turning setbacks into valuable learning opportunities.

Learning from setbacks as opportunities for growth is an essential aspect of sustaining the momentum in change initiatives. This perspective helps in transforming challenges into valuable experiences that contribute to the overall resilience and success of the organization.

Viewing setbacks as learning opportunities requires a shift in mindset. Instead of seeing them as failures or losses, they are perceived as integral parts of the journey toward change. This approach encourages a deeper analysis of what went wrong, fostering a culture of continuous improvement and innovation. When setbacks occur, it's important to conduct thorough debriefings or post-mortems to understand the root causes. These reviews provide insights into the decision-making processes, strategies used, and external factors that might have influenced the outcome. The goal is to extract actionable lessons that can inform future strategies.

Encouraging open and honest discussions about setbacks and their implications is crucial. These discussions should be conducted in a non-judgmental atmosphere where team members feel safe to share their views and insights. This openness fosters a collaborative approach to problem-solving and learning. Documenting the lessons learned from setbacks and sharing them across the organization is another important step. This not only ensures that the knowledge is retained but also helps in preventing the repetition of similar mistakes. Shared learning contributes to the collective intelligence of the organization. Implementing changes based on these lessons is key to turning setbacks into growth opportunities. This might involve adjusting processes, refining strategies, or introducing new practices. The implementation of these changes demonstrates a commitment to learning and improvement.

Setbacks also offer an opportunity to develop resilience and adaptability among team members. Navigating through challenges and finding solutions strengthens the team's ability to handle future obstacles, building a stronger and more adaptable organization. Recognizing and appreciating the effort and learning in the face of setbacks is important. This recognition reinforces a positive approach to handling challenges and motivates team members to continue contributing their best efforts.

Celebrating successes and reinforcing a change culture are key components in sustaining the momentum of change initiatives.

These practices help in embedding the change deeply within the organization and maintaining ongoing support and enthusiasm for the transformation.

Celebrating successes, both big and small, plays a crucial role in maintaining morale and motivation. Acknowledging milestones achieved and goals met serves as positive reinforcement, encouraging continued effort and dedication. These celebrations can be formal events or informal acknowledgments, but their primary purpose is to recognize and appreciate the hard work and progress made. In reinforcing a change culture, it's important to consistently communicate the values and behaviors that align with the change. This involves not just talking about these values but also demonstrating them through actions and decisions. Leaders play a critical role in this by modeling the desired behaviors, setting a clear example for the rest of the organization.

Integrating the change into everyday practices and processes helps in making it a part of the organizational fabric. This might involve updating policies, revising job descriptions, or embedding change-related goals into performance evaluations. Making the change an integral part of the daily operations reinforces its permanence and importance. Providing ongoing training and development supports the reinforcement of the change culture. Continuous learning opportunities help employees to adapt to new ways of working and keep them aligned with the change objectives. This training should be aligned with the needs that arise as the change evolves.

Creating opportunities for employees to share their experiences and stories about the change can also reinforce the culture. Storytelling can be a powerful tool in illustrating the impact of the change and sharing best practices. It helps in making the benefits of the change more tangible and relatable. Regularly soliciting feedback and involving employees in the ongoing development of the change ensures that the change remains relevant and effective. It also fosters a sense of ownership and engagement among employees, making them active participants in the change process. Recognizing and rewarding change champions – individuals who actively support and promote the change – can further reinforce the change culture. These individuals can be instrumental in influencing their peers and contributing to a positive change environment.

Recognizing the significance of celebrating milestones and achievements is a pivotal element in maintaining the momentum of change initiatives. Celebrations not only acknowledge the hard work and commitment of those involved but also serve as important markers of progress, reinforcing the objectives and benefits of the change. Celebrating milestones helps in building a sense of accomplishment and pride among team members. Recognizing the effort put into reaching each milestone instills a sense of achievement, which is crucial for morale. It also serves as a motivational tool, as team members feel their contributions are valued and impactful. These celebrations act as tangible indicators of progress, making the often-abstract concept of change more concrete. They provide an opportunity to reflect on the journey, understand what has been achieved, and what remains to be done. This reflection is important for maintaining a clear focus and direction. In addition to formal achievements, recognizing the less visible, day-to-day efforts that contribute to the change can be equally important. Acknowledging these efforts ensures that even the smaller, incremental steps are valued, which is essential for sustaining long-term commitment to the change.

Celebrations can also serve as an opportunity for team-building and strengthening relationships. Bringing people together in a positive and informal setting can foster a sense of community and solidarity, which is beneficial for collaborative work environments. Incorporating storytelling into these celebrations can amplify their impact. Sharing stories of challenges overcome, innovative solutions, and personal growth experienced through the change process can inspire and encourage others. It helps in illustrating the real-world impact and benefits of the change. Celebrating success also provide an opportunity to reiterate the vision and goals of the change initiative. They can be used as platforms to communicate the next steps and what is expected moving forward, thus aligning everyone towards the continued journey of change. Celebrating milestones and achievements helps in creating a culture that values progress and change. It demonstrates that the organization is committed to acknowledging and appreciating the efforts made towards achieving its goals, thereby fostering a positive and progressive organizational culture.

Building a culture that values and supports ongoing change is fundamental for the longevity and effectiveness of any transformation initiative. Such a culture not only embraces change but also sees it as an essential aspect of growth and development. Establishing this culture starts with leadership. Leaders must embody and promote a mindset that values adaptability, flexibility, and continuous improvement. By demonstrating a positive attitude towards change and being open to new ideas and approaches, leaders set a tone that permeates throughout the organization.

Communication plays a critical role in building this culture. Regularly communicating the benefits of change, sharing success stories, and discussing the lessons learned from setbacks help in fostering a positive perception of change. It's important to ensure that the narrative around change is constructive and focused on the long-term benefits it brings. Involving employees in the change process is key to making them feel valued and heard. When employees have a say in how changes are implemented, they are more likely to support and embrace them. This involvement can range from giving feedback to being part of decision-making processes or change implementation teams.

Training and development are also essential in cultivating a change-friendly culture. Providing employees with the skills and knowledge they need to navigate change effectively empowers them to be proactive participants rather than passive observers. Recognizing and rewarding flexibility, adaptability, and innovative thinking reinforces the value placed on these traits. When employees see that their efforts to embrace and drive change are acknowledged and appreciated, it encourages these behaviors.

Creating an environment that tolerates risk and learns from failure is crucial. A culture that supports ongoing change is one where mistakes are seen as opportunities for learning and growth, not reasons for punishment or criticism. Fostering collaboration and cross-functional teamwork can also support a change-oriented culture. When employees work together across departments or specialties, it breaks down silos and encourages a more holistic and adaptable approach to how work is done.

Regularly reviewing and updating policies, processes, and practices to align with the evolving needs of the organization and its environment ensures that the culture remains relevant and conducive to change. Reinforcing change behaviors and practices to make them habitual is crucial in ensuring the lasting impact of change initiatives. This process involves embedding new behaviors and practices into the daily routines and culture of the organization so that they become second nature to its members.

Consistent reinforcement is key to making new behaviors habitual. This can be achieved through continuous messaging, reminders, and incorporating these behaviors into regular processes and procedures. It's important to consistently highlight how these behaviors align with the organization's goals and values. Leadership plays a pivotal role in this reinforcement. Leaders must model the desired behaviors consistently, demonstrating their commitment to the change. When leaders exemplify the change, it sends a powerful message to the rest of the organization and sets a standard for others to follow.

Training and development initiatives are important tools for reinforcing change behaviors. Regular training sessions help keep the new practices fresh in employees' minds and provide opportunities to refine and improve these skills. Training should be an ongoing process, not just a one-time event at the beginning of the change initiative. Feedback mechanisms, such as surveys, feedback sessions, and performance reviews, can be used to monitor how well the new behaviors are being adopted and to identify areas where additional support might be needed. Positive feedback and constructive criticism can guide employees in making the necessary adjustments to their behaviors.

Recognition and reward systems can be powerful motivators in reinforcing change behaviors. Acknowledging and rewarding individuals and teams who consistently exhibit the desired behaviors encourages others to emulate them. This can be through formal recognition programs or informal methods, such as verbal praise or team celebrations. Peer influence and social proof are also effective in making change behaviors habitual. Encouraging the sharing of success stories and best practices among employees can inspire others to adopt the new behaviors. Seeing peers succeed with the new behaviors reinforces the idea that these changes are beneficial and achievable.

Creating supportive environments where employees feel safe to experiment with new behaviors and practices is essential. This includes providing the necessary resources, time, and support for employees to adapt to the new ways of working. Regular reviews and adjustments of the change initiatives ensure that the behaviors and practices remain relevant and effective. As the organization and its environment evolve, so too should the behaviors and practices that were introduced during the change.

Learning from both successful and failed change initiatives is an invaluable process in the journey of organizational transformation. It involves analyzing and understanding what worked and what didn't, to refine future strategies and approaches. This dual perspective ensures a well-rounded and informed approach to managing change. Successful change initiatives provide models of what works. Analyzing these successes helps identify best practices, effective strategies, and tactics that were instrumental in achieving the desired outcomes. It's important to understand the factors that contributed to the success, such as leadership styles, communication approaches, stakeholder engagement, and the methods used to overcome resistance. Failed change initiatives, while often viewed negatively, are rich sources of learning. They offer insights into potential pitfalls, ineffective strategies, and unforeseen challenges. Analyzing failures helps in understanding the mistakes and miscalculations that occurred, providing crucial lessons on what to avoid in future initiatives.

Documenting and sharing the learnings from both successes and failures is vital. This can be done through case studies, debrief sessions, or learning workshops. The goal is to disseminate the knowledge gained throughout the organization, turning individual experiences into collective wisdom. Encouraging a culture that values learning from experience is crucial. This culture should celebrate successes and view failures not as sources of blame, but as opportunities for growth. Such an environment encourages openness and honesty, making it easier for teams to share their experiences and learn from each other.

Cross-functional learning is also important. Often, lessons from change initiatives can be applicable across different departments or units within the organization. Facilitating cross-functional discussions and learning sessions can help spread the benefits of these insights more widely. Leaders should actively participate in the learning process, both by sharing their own experiences and by encouraging their teams to reflect on and learn from both successes and failures. Leadership engagement demonstrates the value placed on continuous learning and improvement.

Reflection and adaptation are key components of learning from change initiatives. It involves not just understanding what happened and why, but also how to adapt strategies and approaches based on these learnings. This reflective practice should be an ongoing process, integrated into the organization's approach to change management. Retrospective analysis in change initiatives is a powerful tool for understanding the dynamics of organizational transformation. It involves looking back at the change process to evaluate what went well, what didn't, and why. This reflection is invaluable for learning and improving future change efforts. The primary value of retrospective analysis lies in its ability to provide a clear, comprehensive view of the entire change process. By stepping back and reviewing the initiative from start to finish, organizations can gain insights into the effectiveness of their strategies, the appropriateness of their methods, and the impact of their actions.

Retrospective analysis helps in identifying successful elements of the change process. This could include effective communication strategies, strong leadership, efficient resource allocation, or innovative problem-solving approaches. Understanding these success factors allows organizations to replicate and build upon them in future initiatives. Equally important is the analysis of areas that did not go as planned. Retrospective analysis can reveal weaknesses in planning, gaps in stakeholder engagement, resource shortfalls, or unforeseen external influences. Acknowledging and understanding these shortcomings is crucial for avoiding similar issues in subsequent changes.

Engaging a diverse group of stakeholders in the retrospective analysis can enhance its value. Different perspectives provide a more holistic understanding of the change process, capturing insights that might be overlooked by a single group or individual. Retrospective analysis also fosters a learning culture within the organization. It demonstrates a commitment to continuous improvement and signals that the organization values learning from both its successes and its challenges. This culture encourages openness, adaptability, and innovation.

Documenting the findings from retrospective analyses is vital. This documentation becomes a part of the organization's knowledge base, serving as a reference for future change initiatives. It can guide decision-making, strategy development, and execution in future projects. The value of retrospective analysis extends beyond specific change initiatives. It contributes to the development of organizational wisdom and maturity, enhancing the overall capacity of the organization to manage change effectively.

Extracting lessons from both successful and unsuccessful change efforts is a critical step in the journey of continuous improvement within an organization. This reflective practice involves delving into the details of past initiatives to understand what led to their outcomes. From successful endeavors, it's about distilling the key factors that contributed to their success, such as effective communication, strong leadership, stakeholder engagement, and efficient resource management. These elements become the building blocks for replicating success in future change efforts.

Conversely, learning from unsuccessful change efforts is equally important. It requires an honest assessment of what went wrong. This might involve recognizing missteps in planning, execution, or perhaps underestimating the resistance to change. Understanding these pitfalls provides invaluable insights that can prevent future initiatives from encountering similar obstacles.

The process of extracting these lessons should be inclusive and involve participants from various levels of the organization. This inclusive approach ensures a comprehensive perspective, capturing insights from those who were directly involved in the change process as well as those who were affected by it. Once these lessons are identified, the next step is applying the insights gained to future initiatives. This application is not just a reactive adjustment to past mistakes but a proactive strategy to enhance the organization's change management capabilities. It involves integrating these learnings into the planning and implementation phases of future change projects, adjusting methodologies, and refining strategies based on past experiences.

Applying these insights also means continuously updating the organization's change management frameworks and practices. It involves training and developing staff, updating policies, and possibly even altering organizational structures to better support change. By doing so, the organization not only learns from its past but also evolves, becoming more adept at handling change. These insights can help in predicting and navigating future challenges more effectively. They equip the organization with a more nuanced understanding of how change unfolds within its unique context, enabling a more tailored and effective approach to managing change.

Finishing the chapter with the emphasis on extracting lessons from both successful and unsuccessful change efforts and applying insights gained from past experiences to future initiatives highlights the importance of learning as a continuous process. This learning is integral to building a resilient, adaptable, and forward-looking organization, capable of navigating the complexities of change with greater confidence and success.

Chapter 7: Building a Change Culture

Building a change-friendly organizational culture is a strategic imperative in today's fast-paced and ever-evolving business environment. The significance of such a culture lies in its ability to empower an organization to respond swiftly and effectively to emerging challenges and opportunities. This adaptability is crucial for long-term success and sustainability. A change-friendly culture fosters an atmosphere where innovation and creativity are encouraged, making the organization more dynamic and forward-thinking. In such an environment, employees are not just open to new ideas and approaches but are actively seeking them out. This mindset is vital for staying ahead in competitive markets and for continuous improvement. A culture that embraces change is better equipped to handle the uncertainties and complexities of the modern business world. It allows the organization to pivot quickly in response to new market trends, technological advancements, and changes in customer preferences, maintaining its relevance and competitiveness.

In a change-friendly culture, employees feel more engaged and empowered. When change is part of the organizational DNA, employees are more likely to contribute their ideas and play an active role in the transformation processes. This engagement leads to higher job satisfaction, better performance, and a stronger commitment to the organization. Such a culture also helps in attracting and retaining talent. Professionals, especially those from younger generations, often seek dynamic and progressive work environments where they can grow and make a meaningful impact. An organization that is known for its adaptability and openness to change is more attractive to these individuals.

An adaptive culture also contributes to the resilience of the organization. It helps in building a workforce that is not just equipped to handle change but can thrive in it. This resilience is invaluable in navigating through periods of uncertainty and disruption. The development of an adaptive culture also has a positive impact on the organization's reputation. It positions the organization as a leader and an innovator in its field, enhancing its appeal to customers, partners, and investors.

The significance of a change-friendly organizational culture lies in its contribution to the organization's adaptability, innovation, employee engagement, talent attraction, resilience, and overall reputation. Cultivating such a culture is not just about responding to immediate changes but about embedding a mindset that ensures the organization remains vibrant, relevant, and successful in the long term. Fostering a culture that embraces change as a norm involves a comprehensive strategy focused on reshaping attitudes, behaviors, and organizational practices. This approach is essential for creating an environment where change is viewed as a regular and positive aspect of the organizational life.

1. Leadership Commitment and Role Modeling: Change culture starts at the top. Leaders must not only advocate for change but also embody it. By demonstrating flexibility, openness to new ideas, and a willingness to challenge the status quo, leaders can inspire similar behaviors throughout the organization.

2. Effective Communication of Change Benefits: Regularly communicate the positive aspects of change, including how it contributes to the organization's success and personal growth opportunities for employees. Highlighting real examples of successful changes helps in illustrating these benefits.

3. Employee Involvement and Empowerment: Actively involve employees in the change process from the outset. This can include idea generation, planning, and implementation. Empowering employees to contribute and make decisions fosters a sense of ownership and commitment to the change.

4. Training and Development: Provide ongoing learning opportunities that focus on developing skills necessary for adapting to change. This includes problem-solving, critical thinking, and adaptability. Training should also address how to cope with change-related stress and uncertainty.

5. Creating a Safe Environment for Experimentation: Encourage a culture where experimentation and calculated risk-taking are supported. Ensure that failures are not punished but viewed as learning opportunities. This environment promotes innovation and creativity, essential elements of a change-friendly culture.

6. Recognition and Reward for Change Champions: Acknowledge and reward individuals and teams who embrace and champion change. Recognition programs can be formal, like awards or promotions, or informal, such as public acknowledgment in meetings or internal communications.

7. Regular Feedback and Dialogue: Establish mechanisms for regular feedback on change initiatives. Create forums for open dialogue where employees can express their thoughts and concerns about changes, ensuring that their voices are heard and considered.

8. Flexibility in Policies and Procedures: Review and adjust organizational policies and procedures to support the change-friendly culture. This includes creating more flexible work arrangements, revising performance metrics, and streamlining processes to encourage quick and effective response to change.

9. Celebrating Milestones and Successes: Regularly celebrate milestones and successes in the change journey. This not only reinforces the positive aspects of change but also helps in building momentum and enthusiasm for future initiatives.

10. Continuous Assessment and Adaptation: Regularly assess the organization's culture and readiness for change. Be prepared to adapt strategies as needed based on feedback and changing

circumstances. Continuous assessment ensures that the strategies remain effective and relevant.

Fostering a culture that embraces change as a norm involves leadership role modeling, effective communication of change benefits, employee involvement, training and development, creating a safe environment for experimentation, recognition of change champions, regular feedback and dialogue, flexibility in policies, celebrating successes, and continuous assessment and adaptation. These strategies collectively create an organizational environment where change is not only accepted but is actively welcomed and leveraged for growth and innovation.

Cultivating a mindset where change is seen as an opportunity rather than a disruption is a fundamental step in fostering a culture that embraces change. This shift in perspective transforms how individuals and the organization as a whole perceive and respond to change. To cultivate this mindset, it's essential to start by redefining the narrative around change. Instead of framing change as a challenge or a threat, it should be presented as a chance for growth, innovation, and improvement. This redefinition helps in altering the initial emotional and psychological responses to change.

Encouraging curiosity and a thirst for learning within the organization plays a significant role in this process. When employees are curious, they are more likely to explore new ideas, ask questions, and seek out new solutions, viewing change as a pathway to learning and personal development. Leadership is instrumental in fostering this mindset. When leaders approach change with enthusiasm and a positive attitude, it sets a tone for the rest of the organization. They should share their vision of how change can lead to better outcomes, both for the organization and its employees.

Providing real-life examples of how change has positively impacted the organization or other organizations can also reinforce this perspective. Success stories, case studies, and testimonials about the benefits of embracing change can be powerful tools in shifting perceptions. Creating opportunities for employees to contribute to change initiatives helps them see change as something they have a stake in rather than something imposed upon them. Involvement in the change process gives employees a sense of control and ownership, which can transform their perception of change.

Embedding this mindset into training and development programs ensures that it becomes an integral part of the organizational culture. This includes offering training sessions that focus on adaptability, resilience, and innovative thinking. Acknowledging and celebrating adaptability and resilience reinforces the idea that these traits are valued and rewarded in the organization. Recognizing employees who adapt well to change encourages others to adopt a similar outlook. Open communication about the benefits and challenges of change is crucial. It's important to address concerns and fears honestly while also highlighting the potential opportunities that change brings. This open dialogue can help in balancing the narrative around change, making it more nuanced and realistic.

Cultivating a mindset where change is seen as an opportunity involves redefining the narrative around change, encouraging curiosity and learning, leadership modeling, sharing success stories, involving employees in change processes, integrating the mindset into training programs, acknowledging adaptability, and maintaining open communication. These practices collectively help shift the organizational culture to one that views change not as a disruption but as a valuable opportunity for growth and improvement.

Understanding individual preferences in change interactions is a critical aspect of building a change-friendly culture. It acknowledges that each employee may respond differently to change based on their personality, experiences, and work style. Tailoring change strategies to accommodate these diverse preferences can significantly enhance the effectiveness and acceptance of organizational transformations. Recognizing the diversity in responses to change is the first step. Employees can range from early adopters, who are eager and excited about new challenges, to more cautious individuals who may be resistant or anxious about change. Understanding these different responses is key to addressing their specific needs and concerns.

Effective communication plays a vital role in understanding individual preferences. This involves not just disseminating information but also actively listening to employees' feedback and concerns. Such two-way communication allows leaders to gauge individual reactions and tailor their approach accordingly. Personalized support is crucial in managing diverse responses to change. For some employees, additional training and reassurance might be necessary, while others may require more autonomy and responsibility to embrace the change. Offering support that aligns with individual needs can help in easing the transition.

Involving employees in the change process can also cater to individual preferences. By giving employees a voice in how change is implemented, they are more likely to feel valued and understood. This involvement can range from participating in decision-making to being part of focus groups or feedback sessions. Leadership styles may need to be adaptable to suit different individuals. Some employees might respond better to a directive approach, while others may prefer a more collaborative style. Leaders who can adjust their style to meet the needs of their team members are more likely to successfully navigate the complexities of change.

Offering resources and tools that cater to diverse learning and working styles is another important aspect. This might include a mix of digital and in-person training, interactive workshops, or self-paced learning modules. Providing a variety of resources ensures that all employees can engage with the change in a way that suits them best. Regular check-ins and follow-ups can help in understanding how individuals are coping with the change over time. These check-ins provide an opportunity to address ongoing concerns, offer additional support, and make adjustments as needed.

Creating a culture of empathy and understanding is essential. Encouraging an environment where differences are respected and valued helps in building trust and openness, making it easier for employees to adapt to and embrace change. Understanding individual preferences in change interactions involves recognizing the diversity in responses to change, effective two-way communication, personalized support, employee involvement, adaptable leadership styles, offering varied resources and tools, regular check-ins, and fostering a culture of empathy. By addressing these individual differences, organizations can create a more inclusive and effective approach to managing change.

Recognizing the diversity of responses to change among individuals is a critical component in building a change culture that is both effective and inclusive. Change affects people differently, and understanding this diversity is key to managing change in a way that respects and addresses the varied needs and reactions of employees. Individual responses to change can vary widely based on a range of factors, including personal experiences, attitudes towards risk, comfort with uncertainty, and the perceived impact of the change on one's role. Some employees might see change as an exciting opportunity for growth and learning, while others may perceive it as a threat to their comfort and stability.

It's important for leaders and change managers to acknowledge that these diverse responses are normal and valid. Recognizing that there is no one-size-fits-all approach to managing change is the first step in addressing these varied reactions effectively. Understanding individual responses requires active listening and empathy. Engaging in open and honest conversations with employees about their feelings and concerns regarding the change can provide valuable insights into their perspectives. It helps in identifying potential areas of resistance and opportunities for support.

Adapting change management strategies to accommodate these diverse responses is crucial. For some employees, additional information and reassurance about the change might be needed.

For others, being involved in the change process or having a say in how the change is implemented can help in easing their concerns. Training and development programs can also be tailored to suit different learning styles and levels of comfort with change. Offering a variety of training methods, such as workshops, e-learning, and one-on-one coaching, ensures that all employees have access to the support they need.

Leaders and change agents should be equipped with the skills to recognize and manage diverse reactions to change. This includes training in emotional intelligence, communication skills, and conflict resolution. Creating a supportive environment where employees feel safe to express their concerns and ask questions is also important. An environment that fosters open dialogue and respects diverse viewpoints encourages employees to engage more fully with the change process. Celebrating the successes and contributions of all employees, regardless of their initial response to the change, reinforces a positive message about the value of diversity in the workplace. It helps in building a culture where different perspectives are seen as an asset, rather than a challenge.

Tailoring change strategies to accommodate varying preferences is an essential approach in building a successful and inclusive change culture. It involves customizing the methods and tactics of change management to align with the diverse needs and comfort levels of different individuals within the organization. This personalized approach recognizes that a uniform strategy may not be effective for everyone, and that flexibility and adaptation are key to successful change implementation. To effectively tailor change strategies, it's crucial to first understand the unique preferences, strengths, and challenges of the workforce. This understanding can be gleaned through surveys, interviews, and open forums where employees are encouraged to share their thoughts and feelings about change. Gathering this data provides a foundation for developing a nuanced and responsive change strategy. Different communication styles and channels may be required to reach and resonate with various groups within the organization. For some, detailed written communication may be most effective, while others may prefer interactive sessions or visual presentations. Offering a variety of communication methods ensures that everyone receives the message in a way that is most meaningful to them.

Involving employees in the planning and implementation of change initiatives can also be tailored to individual preferences. Some may wish to be involved in decision-making processes, while others may prefer to contribute to more operational or feedback-oriented roles. Providing multiple avenues for involvement allows employees to engage with the change in a way that aligns with their preferences and strengths. Training and development programs should be customized to address different learning styles and levels of change readiness. Offering a range of training formats, from in-person workshops to online modules, caters to diverse preferences and ensures that all employees have the necessary skills and knowledge to navigate the change.

Flexibility in the pace and approach of implementing change can also be critical. While some employees may adapt quickly to new systems or processes, others may require more time and gradual transition. Adjusting the pace to accommodate these differences can help in reducing resistance and enhancing overall acceptance of the change. Providing varied types of support throughout the change process is another aspect of tailoring strategies. This could include one-on-one coaching for those who need more personalized guidance, group sessions for collaborative problem-solving, or self-service resources for those who prefer to work independently.

Leaders and change managers should be equipped to recognize and respond to diverse needs and preferences. Training in areas such as emotional intelligence, cultural competency, and adaptive leadership can be valuable in helping leaders to effectively tailor their change strategies. Creating inclusive approaches to change interactions is fundamental in establishing a change culture that is respectful, effective, and embraces the diversity within an organization. Inclusivity in change management ensures that all voices are heard, all concerns are considered, and that the change process is relevant and accessible to everyone involved.

To develop inclusive change interactions, it's important to start by recognizing and valuing the diversity within the organization. This includes not just demographic diversity but also diversity in perspectives, experiences, and ways of thinking. Acknowledging this diversity sets the stage for an inclusive approach. Ensuring representation from all parts of the organization in the change process is key. This representation should include individuals from different departments, roles, levels of seniority, and backgrounds. Such diverse representation ensures that the change strategy is informed by a broad range of insights and experiences.

Communication strategies should be designed to reach and engage everyone. This might involve providing information in multiple languages, using various communication channels, and ensuring that materials are accessible to people with disabilities. The goal is to ensure that no one is left out or disadvantaged in receiving and understanding information about the change. Actively soliciting feedback and input from a wide range of employees is critical. This can be achieved through surveys, focus groups, town hall meetings, and suggestion boxes. Giving everyone an opportunity to share their thoughts and concerns not only provides valuable insights but also helps employees feel valued and involved in the process.

Training and support offered during the change should cater to different learning styles and needs. Providing a mix of training formats, such as in-person sessions, online modules, and hands-on workshops, ensures that all employees can engage with the change in a way that suits them best. Creating safe spaces for open and honest conversations about the change is important. These spaces should be free from judgment and retaliation, encouraging employees to express their views and concerns without fear.

Leaders and change agents should be trained in inclusive practices. This includes understanding unconscious biases, cultural competencies, and how to facilitate inclusive dialogues. Leaders who are equipped with these skills can more effectively manage diverse teams through the change process. Regularly reviewing and adjusting the approach to change based on feedback and outcomes is necessary for maintaining inclusivity. This involves being open to changing strategies and tactics if they are found to be excluding or disadvantaging certain groups.

Developing change advocates and champions is a strategic move in cultivating a culture that not only adapts to but also embraces change. These individuals play a crucial role in driving the change process, influencing their peers, and creating a positive momentum within the organization.

1. Identifying Potential Change Champions: The first step is to identify individuals who are enthusiastic about the change and possess the influence, respect, and communication skills necessary to lead others. These individuals can come from any level within the organization and should embody the attitudes and behaviors that the change seeks to promote.

2. Empowering Champions: Once identified, these change champions should be empowered with the knowledge, resources, and authority they need to effectively advocate for the change. This includes providing them with in-depth information about the change initiative, training on change management principles, and the tools necessary to communicate and implement the change.

3. Training and Support: Change champions may require specific training to enhance their leadership and communication skills. They should also be provided with regular support and guidance as they navigate their roles, including addressing any challenges they encounter in the process.

4. Role Clarification: It's important to clearly define the roles and responsibilities of change champions. This includes outlining their specific tasks, such as communicating key messages, providing feedback to the change management team, or mentoring their colleagues through the transition.

5. Creating a Network of Champions: Building a network of change champions across different departments and levels can

enhance the reach and impact of the change initiative. This network can serve as a platform for sharing ideas, strategies, and feedback, creating a collaborative approach to change implementation.

6. Recognition and Reward: Recognizing and rewarding the efforts of change champions is crucial. This recognition can come in various forms, such as public acknowledgment, awards, or career development opportunities. It helps in reinforcing the value the organization places on their role and contributions.

7. Encouraging Peer Influence: Change champions can leverage their influence among peers to foster a positive attitude towards the change. By sharing their experiences, addressing concerns, and demonstrating the benefits of the change, they can play a key role in reducing resistance and increasing support.

8. Feedback Loop: Change champions can also act as a vital feedback loop for the organization's leadership. They can provide insights into how the change is being perceived at different levels and offer suggestions for enhancing its effectiveness.

Change advocates and champions play a pivotal role in driving cultural change within organizations. They act as the catalysts and facilitators of change, bridging the gap between the change initiative and the broader employee base. Their influence and involvement are critical in shaping and steering the organization's culture towards embracing and sustaining change. As visible and active proponents of change, these individuals help to create and maintain momentum. They do this by embodying the change they advocate for, demonstrating the behaviors and attitudes that the new culture values. Their commitment serves as a model for others to follow, showcasing the benefits and positive aspects of the change.

Change advocates and champions are often seen as accessible and relatable figures within the organization, making them effective communicators. They can translate the vision and goals of the change initiative into practical and understandable terms for their peers. This ability to communicate effectively helps in demystifying the change process and addressing any misconceptions or fears. In their role, change advocates and champions also serve as a support resource for their colleagues. They provide guidance, encouragement, and assistance to others in navigating the change process. This support can be especially crucial in times of uncertainty or when the change presents significant challenges to employees.

Being at the forefront, change advocates and champions are well-positioned to gather feedback from various levels within the organization. They can capture the pulse of the workforce, gauging reactions, concerns, and suggestions regarding the change. This feedback is invaluable for the continuous improvement and adaptation of the change strategy. In driving cultural change, these advocates and champions also play a key role in fostering a collaborative environment. They encourage dialogue, promote the sharing of ideas, and facilitate discussions that allow for diverse perspectives to be heard. This collaborative approach is essential for building a sense of ownership and buy-in among employees.

Change advocates and champions often help in breaking down resistance to change. By addressing concerns, sharing success stories, and providing evidence of the change's positive impact, they can mitigate fears and skepticism, helping their colleagues to move from resistance to acceptance and support. Their role extends to reinforcing the new culture once the initial phases of the change have been implemented. By continuing to promote and model the desired behaviors and practices, they help to ensure that the change is not just a temporary shift, but a lasting transformation in the organization's culture.

In the journey of building a change-friendly culture, identifying and nurturing individuals who actively promote change is a critical process. This involves recognizing those within the organization who naturally gravitate towards change and innovation. These change agents or champions are often characterized by their enthusiasm for new ideas, effective communication skills, and an ability to inspire and motivate others. They are typically respected by their peers and have a knack for influencing others positively.

The process begins by spotting those who display leadership qualities and a propensity for embracing change, regardless of their formal position within the organization. These individuals often have a broad network and are seen as credible and trustworthy by their colleagues, making them ideal candidates for driving change across various departments and levels. Once these individuals are identified, the next step is to equip them with the necessary skills and knowledge. This is achieved through targeted training in change management principles, communication strategies, and leadership skills. Additionally, ensuring that they have a thorough understanding of the objectives and expected outcomes of the change initiative is essential for their effectiveness.

Supporting these change agents is also crucial. This support can come from senior leaders and the change management team, providing guidance, resources, and assistance as they navigate their roles. Empowering them with a degree of autonomy to make decisions and take actions that support the change initiative can further enhance their effectiveness and motivation. Facilitating opportunities for these agents to connect and collaborate with each other can also be beneficial. Such networking enables the sharing of ideas, strategies, and experiences, fostering a more cohesive and informed approach to change management.

Regular check-ins and feedback are important in assessing their progress and addressing any challenges they may face. Acknowledging and recognizing their efforts is vital for their continued motivation and development. Considering the role of a change agent as a pathway to personal and professional growth is important. Identifying opportunities for further development and career advancement can reinforce their commitment to driving and sustaining change within the organization.

Empowering advocates and champions to influence and inspire others is a vital aspect of driving successful change within an organization. These individuals can significantly impact the acceptance and success of change initiatives by using their influence to motivate and guide their peers through the transition.

- Provide Them with In-Depth Knowledge: Change advocates and champions should be well-informed about the details of the change initiative. Providing them with comprehensive knowledge about the reasons for the change, its benefits, and how it will be implemented enables them to confidently and accurately communicate with others.

- Equip Them with Effective Communication Skills: Equipping change advocates with strong communication skills is crucial. Training in areas such as persuasive communication, storytelling, and active listening can enhance their ability to engage effectively with their colleagues and articulate the vision of the change in a compelling manner.

- Grant Authority and Visibility: For advocates and champions to be effective, they need to be given a certain level of authority and visibility within the organization. This could involve public endorsement by senior leaders, formal recognition of their role, and involvement in decision-making processes related to the change.

- Create Platforms for Sharing: Establish platforms where change advocates can share their insights, experiences, and success stories. This could be through internal social media channels, company meetings, newsletters, or informal gatherings. Such platforms allow them to reach a wider audience and serve as a source of inspiration and motivation for others.

- Encourage Peer-to-Peer Engagement: Encourage change advocates to engage directly with their peers. This can include one-on-one conversations, leading small group discussions, or facilitating workshops. Peer-to-peer engagement can be a powerful tool for addressing concerns and building support for the change.

- Support Their Initiatives: Provide support for initiatives undertaken by change advocates. This support can be in the form of resources, time, or guidance. When advocates feel supported in their efforts, they are more likely to take proactive steps in driving change.

- Offer Continuous Training and Development: The role of a change advocate can evolve as the change initiative progresses. Offering continuous training and development opportunities helps them to build their skills and stay effective in their role over time.

- Provide Feedback and Recognition: Regular feedback is important for helping change advocates understand the impact of their efforts and for them to refine their approach. Recognizing their contributions publicly can also boost their morale and reinforce the importance of their role within the organization.

- Encourage Collaborative Problem Solving: Involve change advocates in collaborative problem-solving sessions related to the change. This not only leverages their unique insights but also reinforces their role as key players in the change process.

Ensuring that change becomes an integral part of the organizational DNA is a multifaceted process that requires a strategic approach to embed change deeply and sustainably within the organization. Start by aligning change initiatives with the organization's core values and mission. This alignment ensures that change is not seen as a separate or temporary effort but as a natural extension of the organization's ongoing evolution. It's important to communicate how the change supports and enhances the organization's fundamental principles and goals.

Leadership commitment and modeling are critical in making change a part of the organizational DNA. Leaders should consistently demonstrate the behaviors and attitudes associated with the change, reinforcing its importance and legitimacy. Their actions and decisions should reflect the change principles, setting a clear example for the rest of the organization. Integrate change into all levels of the organization. This means incorporating change-related objectives and behaviors into job descriptions, performance evaluations, and promotion criteria. By doing so, change becomes a criterion for success and advancement within the organization.

Develop policies and procedures that support the change. This could involve revising existing policies or creating new ones that facilitate the desired behaviors and practices. Ensuring that operational guidelines and processes are in sync with the change objectives helps in institutionalizing the change. Engage employees at all levels in the change process. This involves not just informing them about the change but actively involving them in implementing it. Encourage employee input and feedback and provide opportunities for them to contribute to the change process. This involvement fosters a sense of ownership and commitment to the change.

Regular training and development programs are essential to reinforce the change and develop the required skills and knowledge. Continuous learning opportunities help employees adapt to the new ways of working and keep them aligned with the change objectives. Measure and monitor the impact of the change. Use metrics and key performance indicators to assess how the change is affecting various aspects of the organization. This ongoing evaluation helps in understanding the effectiveness of the change and identifying areas for improvement.

Celebrate successes and milestones related to the change. Recognizing and celebrating achievements helps in reinforcing the value of the change and its benefits. It also maintains enthusiasm and commitment to the ongoing change process.

Leveraging instruments and tools for institutionalizing change within organizations is crucial for embedding new processes, behaviors, and mindsets into the organizational fabric. These tools and resources help in making the change more structured, trackable, and sustainable over time.

1. Change Management Software: Platforms like Prosci's ADKAR Model or Kotter's Change Management Software offer robust features for planning, executing, monitoring, and reporting on change initiatives. For example, Prosci's toolset includes assessments, planning templates, and progress tracking features, facilitating better coordination and communication across an organization.

2. Performance Management Systems: Updating systems such as Oracle's Performance Management or SAP SuccessFactors to reflect new change-related goals and objectives can institutionalize change. By aligning individual performance metrics with the desired outcomes of the change, these systems reinforce new behaviors and practices.

3. Internal Communication Platforms: Platforms like Slack or Microsoft Teams ensure consistent and widespread dissemination of information related to the change. These tools can be used for updates, sharing success stories, and reinforcing key messages, as seen in companies like IBM and Google, where internal communication is pivotal to their change strategies.

4. Training and Development Programs: Online learning platforms like LinkedIn Learning or Coursera offer a variety of modules for equipping employees with the skills required for new ways of working. These platforms provide flexibility and a wide range of topics, from leadership to technical skills, essential for supporting change.

5. Feedback and Survey Tools: Tools like SurveyMonkey or Google Forms facilitate the collection of feedback. These platforms are used by organizations to gauge employee sentiments and reactions to the change, enabling ongoing adjustments to the change strategy.

6. Collaboration Tools: Software like Asana or Trello supports new ways of working and encourages teamwork aligned with change initiatives. These tools are used for project management, allowing teams to collaborate effectively and stay aligned with change objectives.

7. Recognition and Reward Systems: Systems that recognize and reward change-related behaviors and achievements are crucial. For instance, Salesforce uses a recognition system that includes awards and acknowledgments in company meetings, reinforcing the importance of adapting to change.

8. Data Analytics Tools: Analytics tools like Tableau or Google Analytics provide insights into the impact of changes. By analyzing data related to productivity, engagement, and other relevant metrics, organizations can understand the effectiveness of their change efforts.

9. Change Advocacy Groups: Establishing formal groups or committees, similar to Google's gTeams or Apple's cross-functional teams, dedicated to advocating and guiding change can be powerful. These groups provide support, share best practices, and help maintain the momentum of the change, ensuring its success and sustainability.

These tools and resources, when effectively leveraged, play a significant role in institutionalizing change within organizations. They not only structure and track the progress of change initiatives but also ensure that these changes become embedded in the organizational DNA, leading to lasting transformation. Creating mechanisms to sustain the change culture over time involves implementing a series of strategic actions and policies that continuously reinforce and support the desired cultural shift. It's about ensuring that the changes become deeply ingrained and enduring aspects of the organization.

One effective approach is the integration of change objectives into the organization's strategic planning process. This ensures that change initiatives are aligned with the long-term goals and vision of the organization, making them fundamental to its direction and success. Regularly reviewing and updating the organization's policies, procedures, and practices to reflect the change culture is also crucial. This might include revising HR policies, operational guidelines, and communication strategies to ensure they are consistent with the new norms and values.

Ongoing training and development are vital to sustain the change culture. Continuous learning opportunities should be provided to employees to keep them updated on new skills, technologies, and methodologies related to the change. This also helps in reinforcing the importance of adaptability and growth. Maintaining open channels of communication is key to sustaining a change-friendly culture. Regular updates about the progress of change initiatives, success stories, and lessons learned should be shared across the organization. This transparency helps in keeping the momentum alive and encourages a sense of collective journey.

Establishing metrics and key performance indicators to measure the impact of the change culture is important. Regularly tracking these metrics helps in understanding the effectiveness of the change initiatives and guides future improvements. Creating forums for feedback and discussion allows employees to voice their opinions and suggestions regarding the change. This could be through regular surveys, town hall meetings, or focus groups. Such forums foster a sense of participation and ownership among employees.

Recognizing and celebrating achievements related to the change culture reinforces its value. Regular acknowledgments, rewards, and celebrations of milestones help in keeping the spirit of the change alive and appreciated. Leadership plays a continuous role in modeling the change culture. Leaders should consistently demonstrate the behaviors and attitudes associated with the new culture, reinforcing its importance and legitimacy. Developing a culture of continuous improvement ensures that the organization remains adaptable and responsive to future changes. Encouraging innovation, experimentation, and learning from both successes and failures keeps the culture dynamic and evolving.

Chapter 8: Learning from Change Pioneers

This chapter opens with an exploration of case studies featuring change pioneers – leaders and organizations renowned for successfully navigating and effecting significant transformations. Through these case studies, we gain an intimate understanding of the strategies, challenges, and triumphs that these pioneers encountered. These stories not only serve as sources of inspiration, but also as practical guides filled with actionable lessons. They offer a window into the real-world application of change theories and principles, providing a tangible context to the abstract aspects of change management.

The success stories of change pioneers vary widely, reflecting the diverse nature of change initiatives across different industries and environments. These case studies also highlight smaller scale yet equally impactful transformations within non-profit organizations, governmental agencies, and startups. They illustrate how effective change management principles are universal and adaptable to various scales and contexts. We will look at how these pioneers identified the need for change, crafted their vision, engaged their stakeholders, overcame resistance, and ultimately embedded the change into their organizational fabric.

The analysis of these case studies is designed to distill practical wisdom and lessons that can be applied in various organizational settings. Readers are encouraged to draw parallels between these stories and their own experiences, extracting relevant strategies and ideas that can be tailored to their unique change initiatives.

Case Examples in Brief

One notable example is the transformation journey of Microsoft under the leadership of Satya Nadella. Upon taking the helm,

Nadella shifted Microsoft's focus from a primarily Windows-centric model to a cloud-first, mobile-first approach. This pivot required not just technological innovation but also a significant cultural shift within the organization.

Another example is the radical transformation of Netflix from a DVD rental service to a streaming giant and content creator. This change was driven by foresight and adaptability, demonstrating how understanding and anticipating market trends can be pivotal in an organization's survival and growth.

The turnaround story of LEGO is also a remarkable case of change management. Faced with financial struggles and a loss of market relevance, LEGO restructured its operations, refocused on core product lines, and engaged more actively with its customer base, resulting in a dramatic revival of the brand.

IBM's shift from a hardware-centric business to a focus on software and services under the leadership of Lou Gerstner in the 1990s is another classic example. This transformation involved not only changing the company's product offerings but also altering its corporate culture and approach to customer service.

The successful rebranding and market expansion of Old Spice by Procter & Gamble showcase how change management can be effectively applied in marketing and brand positioning. By redefining its target audience and revamping its advertising approach, Old Spice significantly broadened its appeal and market share.

1. The Transformation Journey of Microsoft under Satya Nadella

The transformation of Microsoft under Satya Nadella is a notable example of how visionary leadership can redefine an organization's trajectory. When Nadella took over as CEO in 2014, he was faced with the challenge of revitalizing a tech giant that was perceived as losing its edge in an increasingly mobile and cloud-based world.

Nadella's vision was to shift Microsoft from a primarily Windows-centric model to a cloud-first, mobile-first approach. This strategic pivot was not just about altering the company's product offerings but also about transforming its core philosophy and culture.

One of the first major changes was the development and enhancement of Microsoft's cloud computing service, Azure. Nadella's focus on cloud computing was a significant shift from the company's traditional reliance on software sales. Azure soon emerged as a leader in the cloud services market, competing with giants like Amazon Web Services and Google Cloud.

In parallel, there was a strong emphasis on mobile technologies and applications. Recognizing the burgeoning mobile market, Microsoft began to invest more heavily in developing apps and services for a variety of mobile platforms, rather than solely focusing on Windows.

Beyond technological innovation, Nadella initiated a profound cultural shift within Microsoft. He encouraged a mindset of 'learn-it-all' rather than 'know-it-all,' fostering an environment of continuous learning and growth. This cultural shift was pivotal in driving innovation and adaptability among employees.

Nadella also prioritized collaboration and inclusivity, breaking down silos within the organization. He championed the idea of working synergistically and leveraging the diverse strengths of the workforce. This approach not only improved internal collaboration but also led to more integrated and innovative product development.

Under Nadella's leadership, Microsoft also embraced partnerships and collaborations with companies that were once considered rivals. This open approach marked a significant shift in Microsoft's strategy, reflecting a broader vision of technology as an ecosystem rather than a battleground.

The impact of this transformation has been significant. Microsoft has not only regained its position as a technology leader but has also seen substantial financial growth. The company's market value and stock price have soared, reflecting investor confidence in the new direction.

The transformation journey of Microsoft under Satya Nadella is a powerful example of how strategic vision, coupled with cultural and technological change, can rejuvenate a global corporation. It underscores the importance of adaptive leadership and an organizational culture that embraces continuous learning and innovation in the face of industry evolution.

2. The Radical Transformation of Netflix

The transformation of Netflix from a DVD rental service to a global streaming giant and influential content creator stands as a textbook example of corporate adaptability and foresight. This journey is a testament to how understanding and anticipating market trends can be crucial for an organization's survival and growth.

When Netflix was founded in 1997, it started as a DVD rental by mail service. However, Reed Hastings and Marc Randolph, the founders of Netflix, quickly recognized the potential of the internet to revolutionize the way people access and consume entertainment. This realization marked the beginning of a transformation journey that would reshape the entertainment industry.

In 2007, Netflix made a bold move by introducing streaming services, allowing subscribers to watch TV shows and movies over the internet. This was a significant pivot from its DVD rental model, particularly at a time when streaming technology was still in its infancy. This shift capitalized on the increasing availability of high-speed internet and the growing consumer preference for on-demand content.

The introduction of streaming required not only technological innovations but also a change in business strategy. Netflix had to secure deals with content providers, develop a robust content delivery network, and significantly invest in its IT infrastructure. Netflix's transformation didn't stop at streaming; it further evolved by venturing into content creation. With the launch of its first original series, "House of Cards," in 2013, Netflix disrupted traditional TV production and distribution models. Creating its content allowed Netflix more control over its offerings and helped differentiate its service in a crowded market.

This move into content creation was driven by data analytics. Netflix used data from its millions of subscribers to understand viewing preferences, which informed its decisions about what types of content to produce. This data-driven approach to content creation proved to be highly successful, leading to critically acclaimed series like "Stranger Things" and "The Crown."

The success of Netflix's transformation is evident in its substantial subscriber growth, international expansion, and its impact on the entertainment industry. Netflix's model has challenged traditional cable TV and movie theaters, forcing these industries to adapt and innovate. Netflix's journey highlights the importance of organizational agility. The company's willingness to pivot, experiment, and embrace new technologies has been central to its ability to stay ahead in a rapidly changing industry.

Netflix's transformation from a DVD rental service to a streaming and content creation powerhouse demonstrates the power of foresight, adaptability, and data-driven decision-making. It's a compelling story of how a company can redefine an industry and sustain growth by continuously evolving its business model to stay in tune with changing market dynamics and consumer behaviors.

3. The Turnaround Story of LEGO

The LEGO Group's turnaround is an exemplary case of effective change management, showcasing how a company can revive its fortunes by refocusing on its core strengths and engaging deeply with its customer base. In the early 2000s, LEGO faced significant financial struggles and a loss of market relevance, pushing the company to the brink of bankruptcy.

One of the key issues LEGO faced was over-diversification. The company had expanded into areas such as theme parks, video games, and clothing, which diluted its brand and strained its financial resources. This overreach, coupled with increased competition and changing play habits of children, led to a critical situation.

The turnaround began with the appointment of Jørgen Vig Knudstorp as CEO in 2004. Knudstorp brought a fresh perspective and a focus on operational efficiency. One of his first steps was a thorough analysis of LEGO's financial situation and business model. This analysis revealed that a significant portion of the product line was unprofitable. Knudstorp initiated a major restructuring process. He streamlined operations by cutting costs, selling off non-core assets like the LEGO theme parks, and reducing the workforce. While these were difficult decisions, they were necessary to stabilize the company financially.

More importantly, LEGO refocused on its core product lines: the iconic LEGO bricks and sets. This refocus involved pruning the product portfolio to concentrate on lines that resonated with LEGO's heritage and were popular with customers. The company also improved its supply chain and manufacturing processes, ensuring that popular products were always available to consumers. Another significant part of LEGO's revival strategy was to re-engage with its customer base, especially the dedicated community of adult LEGO fans. LEGO started to actively seek feedback from its fans and incorporated their ideas into new products. This led to the creation of the LEGO Ideas platform, where fans could submit and vote on new set ideas, some of which were turned into commercial products.

LEGO also embraced new marketing strategies, leveraging storytelling and partnerships with popular franchises like Star Wars, Harry Potter, and Batman. These collaborations resulted in highly successful product lines that appealed to both children and adults.

The company's efforts to engage with the digital age were also notable. While initially struggling to find its footing in the digital world, LEGO eventually embraced it by developing video games, mobile apps, and even a highly successful film franchise. These ventures allowed LEGO to stay relevant in an increasingly digital world.

The result of these concerted efforts was a dramatic revival of the LEGO brand. By 2015, LEGO had become the world's largest toy company in terms of revenue, overtaking industry giants like Mattel. The LEGO case is a powerful testament to the effectiveness of focusing on core strengths, engaging with customers, and being adaptable to change.

LEGO's turnaround story is a remarkable example of change management done right. It demonstrates how a focus on core products, operational efficiency, customer engagement, and adaptation to new market realities can lead to a brand's dramatic revival and continued success.

4. IBM's Transformation under Lou Gerstner

The transformation of IBM in the 1990s under the leadership of Lou Gerstner is a classic example of a company successfully navigating a profound shift in its business model and organizational culture. When Gerstner took over as CEO in 1993, IBM was on the brink of disintegration, suffering from significant financial losses and a rapidly changing technology market.

Gerstner's arrival marked the beginning of a pivotal shift from IBM's traditional focus on hardware to a new emphasis on software and services. This strategic shift was driven by a recognition that the technology industry was moving away from a hardware-dominated landscape to one where software solutions and IT services were increasingly valued.

One of the first challenges Gerstner addressed was the organizational structure of IBM. At the time, the company was highly decentralized, with various divisions operating almost independently. Gerstner implemented a more integrated approach, consolidating the company's operations to foster better coordination and a unified strategy. Changing IBM's product offerings involved not only developing new capabilities in software and services but also altering the way the company viewed its market. Gerstner shifted IBM's focus towards providing integrated solutions to complex IT problems, rather than simply selling hardware products. This required a substantial investment in developing the company's expertise in software development, consulting, and IT services.

Perhaps one of the most significant aspects of IBM's transformation under Gerstner was the change in corporate culture. Gerstner recognized that a customer-centric approach was essential for IBM's revival. He pushed for a culture that prioritized customer service and responsiveness, breaking away from the inward-focused, bureaucratic culture that had previously characterized IBM. Under Gerstner's leadership, IBM also revamped its approach to innovation. Rather than focusing solely on technological breakthroughs, the company started to emphasize the practical application of technology to solve real-world business problems. This shift not only aligned IBM with market demands but also fostered a more collaborative and pragmatic approach to innovation.

Gerstner's tenure also saw IBM making strategic acquisitions in the software and IT services sectors, bolstering its capabilities in these areas. These acquisitions were integral to expanding IBM's portfolio and competencies in the rapidly growing field of IT services. The impact of this transformation was profound. IBM successfully reinvented itself, reversing its financial decline and reestablishing its position as a leader in the global technology market. The company's successful pivot from hardware to software and services has been widely studied as a model for how large corporations can adapt to changing industry landscapes.

IBM's transformation under Lou Gerstner in the 1990s is a testament to the power of strategic realignment and cultural change in revitalizing a struggling company. It highlights the importance of customer focus, organizational integration, and a pragmatic approach to innovation in achieving successful business transformation.

5. The Rebranding and Market Expansion of Old Spice

The transformation of Old Spice under the stewardship of Procter & Gamble is a remarkable case study in change management, particularly in the realms of marketing and brand positioning. Once perceived as a brand for an older generation, Old Spice underwent a dramatic rebranding and market expansion that revitalized its image, broadened its appeal, and increased its market share.

Prior to its transformation, Old Spice was often associated with an older demographic, and its market position was stagnating. Recognizing the need for change, Procter & Gamble, which acquired Old Spice in 1990, embarked on a mission to rejuvenate the brand and appeal to a younger, more diverse audience.

The cornerstone of Old Spice's transformation was a bold redefinition of its target audience. Procter & Gamble shifted the brand's focus from older men to a younger, trendier demographic. This repositioning was crucial to tapping into a larger and more dynamic market segment.

Revamping Old Spice's advertising approach played a pivotal role in this transformation. The brand launched a series of innovative, humorous, and edgy marketing campaigns that broke away from traditional masculine stereotypes. The most notable among these was the "The Man Your Man Could Smell Like" campaign, featuring Isaiah Mustafa. This campaign became a viral sensation, significantly elevating the brand's profile and appeal among younger consumers.

These marketing efforts were complemented by a diversification of the product line. Old Spice introduced new product ranges, including body washes and deodorants, catering to the evolving preferences of the younger market. This diversification not only refreshed the brand's image but also helped in capturing a larger share of the grooming market. In addition to traditional advertising, Old Spice leveraged social media platforms to engage directly with consumers. This approach allowed the brand to build a robust online presence, further solidifying its appeal to a tech-savvy, younger audience.

The success of these strategies was evident in the increased market share and brand recognition. Old Spice transformed from a brand perceived as outdated to one that was synonymous with youth, vigor, and humor. Its successful rebranding helped in capturing new customer segments and revitalizing its market presence.

Old Spice's transformation under Procter & Gamble is a testament to the power of effective change management in marketing and brand positioning. It highlights how understanding market trends, redefining target audiences, innovative advertising, product diversification, and effective use of digital platforms can collectively rejuvenate a brand and drive its growth in a competitive market.

In analyzing the change processes of the aforementioned cases – Microsoft, Netflix, LEGO, IBM, and Old Spice – certain patterns and dynamics emerge that provide deeper insights into successful change management.

1. Vision and Leadership: A common thread across these cases is the presence of strong, visionary leadership. Leaders like Satya Nadella, Reed Hastings, and Lou Gerstner played pivotal roles in envisioning the change and steering their organizations through the transformation process. Their leadership was not just about setting a new direction but also about inspiring and motivating their workforce to embrace the change.

2. Adaptability to Market Trends: Each of these companies demonstrated a remarkable ability to adapt to market trends and consumer behaviors. For instance, Netflix's shift to streaming services was a direct response to the evolving way audiences consumed media. Similarly, Old Spice's rebranding efforts were aligned with changing perceptions of masculinity in society. This adaptability was crucial in ensuring their relevance and competitiveness.

3. Customer-Centric Approach: A strong focus on customer needs and preferences was evident in these transformations. LEGO's engagement with its customer base for feedback and product ideas and IBM's shift towards a customer-centric service model exemplify this focus. Understanding and responding to customer needs helped these companies to realign their offerings and strategies effectively.

4. Innovation and Risk-Taking: Innovation played a significant role in these companies' transformation. Netflix's foray into content creation and Old Spice's daring advertising campaigns are examples of innovative strategies that broke industry norms. These moves involved significant risks but ultimately paid off by setting these companies apart from their competitors.

5. Cultural Transformation: Beyond strategic and operational changes, a shift in organizational culture was a key component of these transformations. Microsoft's cultural shift towards a more collaborative and open environment under Nadella and the move by LEGO to foster a culture of innovation and creativity were integral to supporting and sustaining the change.

6. Effective Communication: Effective communication was central to these change processes. Whether it was internally communicating the vision and strategy to employees or externally marketing new brand images to customers, clear and consistent communication helped in gaining buy-in and building momentum for the change.

7. Continuous Evolution: Lastly, these companies did not view change as a one-time event but as an ongoing process. They continuously evolved by reassessing market conditions and internal progress and adjusting their strategies accordingly. This approach of continuous evolution helped them to stay ahead in rapidly changing industries.

The successful change processes of these companies were characterized by visionary leadership, adaptability to market trends, a customer-centric approach, a willingness to innovate and take risks, cultural transformation, effective communication, and a mindset of continuous evolution. These patterns and dynamics offer valuable lessons for organizations looking to embark on their own transformation journeys.

The impact of change pioneers is multifaceted. Firstly, they often drive significant financial turnaround and growth. For example, the strategic changes implemented by Apple under Steve Jobs, which included the introduction of groundbreaking products like the iPhone and the iPad, not only saved the company from near bankruptcy but also catapulted it to unprecedented levels of profitability and market leadership. Change pioneers frequently revolutionize industry standards and consumer expectations. Amazon, under Jeff Bezos, transformed the retail industry with its customer-centric approach, vast selection, and speedy delivery, fundamentally changing how people shop and what they expect from retail services.

In some cases, change pioneers have been responsible for catalyzing technological advancements and innovation. Google's continual evolution, for instance, has significantly shaped the tech industry, influencing areas ranging from online search and advertising to artificial intelligence and cloud computing. Change pioneers also often lead the way in adopting and advocating for sustainable and ethical business practices. The leadership of companies like Patagonia in environmental advocacy and sustainable business practices has not only altered the company's operational approach but also set new industry standards for corporate responsibility.

These leaders can have a lasting impact on organizational culture. Microsoft's shift under Satya Nadella towards a more collaborative and open work culture, emphasizing learning and innovation, is a prime example of how change at the top can permeate an entire organization, affecting employee engagement and productivity. The influence of change pioneers extends beyond immediate organizational or financial success. They often leave a legacy that shapes future leadership styles, business models, and corporate strategies. Their approaches become case studies and blueprints for other leaders and organizations aspiring to adapt and excel in an ever-changing business world. In examining the change processes led by various pioneers across different industries, certain common patterns and dynamics emerge, offering valuable insights into the essence of successful change management.

- Clear Vision and Strategic Direction: Change pioneers consistently exhibit a clear and compelling vision for the future. This vision acts as a north star, guiding the organization through the turbulence of change. Whether it's Steve Jobs' vision for Apple or Howard Schultz's for Starbucks, having a clear strategic direction is crucial for rallying the organization and setting the course for transformation.

- Leadership Commitment and Involvement: Successful change initiatives are often driven by leaders who are deeply committed and actively involved in the change process. These leaders don't just delegate; they are the champions of change, personally invested in seeing the transformation through. This high level of involvement from leadership ensures alignment and commitment throughout the organization.

- Customer and Market Orientation: Pioneers of change maintain a strong focus on the customer and market needs. They constantly gather insights about customer preferences, market trends, and competitive dynamics. This orientation allows them to anticipate changes in the market and adapt their strategies accordingly, as seen in Amazon's customer-centric approach under Jeff Bezos.

- Culture of Innovation and Agility: Change pioneers foster a culture that values innovation, flexibility, and agility. They encourage experimentation, are open to new ideas, and are quick to adapt to changing circumstances. Google's culture of innovation and Facebook's mantra of "move fast and break things" in its early days are examples of such an environment.

- Effective Communication and Stakeholder Engagement: Effective communication is a hallmark of successful change processes. Pioneers ensure that their vision and the reasons for change are communicated clearly and consistently across all levels of the organization. They also engage various stakeholders – employees, customers, and partners – to build support and address concerns.

- Empowering Employees and Encouraging Ownership: Many change leaders empower their employees to take ownership of the change. This empowerment fosters a sense of responsibility and commitment among employees. Toyota's lean manufacturing and the associated practice of Kaizen is an example where employee empowerment is central to continuous improvement.

- Continuous Learning and Adaptation: Successful change processes are characterized by continuous learning and adaptation. Pioneers use feedback loops to learn from successes and failures and are quick to adjust their strategies in response to new information or changing market conditions.

- Balancing Short-Term Needs with Long-Term Goals: While focusing on long-term strategic goals, change pioneers also manage the short-term challenges of change. They balance immediate operational needs with the long-term vision, ensuring that the organization remains stable and functional during the transition period.

Mining the experiences and wisdom of change pioneers is an exercise in understanding the depths of their journeys, extracting valuable lessons from both their successes and their setbacks. These pioneers offer a wealth of knowledge that is instrumental in guiding current and future leaders through their own transformations. Understanding both the triumphs and challenges of these leaders is key. The journey of someone like Howard Schultz, who not only built Starbucks into a global brand but also revitalized it after a downturn, offers profound insights into resilience and strategic foresight. Similarly, the leadership style and decision-making processes of pioneers like Indra Nooyi at PepsiCo can reveal important lessons in visionary leadership and integrating corporate responsibility into the business model.

Adaptability and resilience are recurrent themes in the narratives of these change leaders. Satya Nadella's transformative leadership at Microsoft, for instance, highlights how adaptability can significantly redirect a company's course. The role of innovation and risk-taking is also central to these stories, as illustrated by Jeff Bezos' approach with Amazon, consistently pushing the company into new domains. Effective stakeholder engagement and communication are crucial aspects of these leaders' strategies. How they managed to navigate both internal and external communications offers strategies for effective engagement and messaging. Furthermore, many of these pioneers have led significant cultural transformations within their organizations. Learning from their approaches to changing company culture, as seen in Google's emphasis on openness and innovation, can provide valuable insights.

The use of technology and data in driving change is increasingly relevant in today's digital age. Netflix's use of data analytics to inform its content strategy exemplifies the effective use of technology and data in decision-making. Additionally, the balance between addressing short-term pressures and maintaining a focus on long-term strategic goals is a delicate one. The sustainability initiatives championed by Paul Polman during his time at Unilever underscore the importance of long-term thinking in achieving sustainable business success. In studying the journeys of change pioneers across various industries, we can distill key insights and lessons that are invaluable for anyone embarking on a change management journey. These lessons, drawn from the successes and challenges of these leaders, provide a roadmap for navigating change effectively.

1. Visionary Leadership is Crucial: The importance of having a clear and compelling vision cannot be overstated. Leaders like Steve Jobs and Howard Schultz had a clear vision for the future and were able to articulate this vision in a way that inspired others. A strong vision provides direction and purpose, serving as a guiding light through the complexities of change.

2. Adaptability to Changing Market Dynamics: The ability to adapt to changing market conditions is a defining characteristic of successful change management. Netflix's transition to streaming services in response to changing consumer behaviors exemplifies the need to remain flexible and responsive to external market dynamics.

3. Customer-Centric Approach Drives Success: A deep understanding of and focus on customer needs can guide successful change. Amazon's customer-first approach under Jeff Bezos demonstrates how aligning organizational strategies with customer needs leads to growth and innovation.

4. Cultural Transformation is Fundamental: Change is not just about strategy and operations; it's also about culture. Satya Nadella's emphasis on changing Microsoft's culture to one that values learning and collaboration highlights the need for cultural transformation as part of successful change management.

5. Effective Communication is Key: Clear and consistent communication is essential throughout the change process. It's important not just to communicate the what and the how, but also the why of change, as effective communication builds trust and reduces resistance.

6. Employee Engagement and Empowerment: Engaging employees in the change process and empowering them to contribute can lead to more successful outcomes. When employees feel part of the change process, they are more likely to support and drive the change.

7. Innovation and Risk-Taking: Embracing innovation and being willing to take calculated risks can lead to significant rewards. Companies like Google have thrived by continually innovating and not being afraid to venture into new territories.

8. Balancing Short-Term Challenges with Long-Term Vision: Successful change management involves managing the immediate, operational challenges while keeping an eye on the long-term strategic goals. This balance is critical to ensure that the organization navigates through change without losing sight of its ultimate objectives.

9. Continuous Learning and Improvement: Change is not a one-time event but an ongoing process. The most successful change leaders foster a culture of continuous learning and improvement within their organizations.

10. Data-Driven Decision Making: Utilizing data to inform decisions is increasingly important. Netflix's use of data analytics for content creation and customer engagement is a prime example of data-driven decision making in action.

These key insights and lessons from the journeys of change pioneers provide a blueprint for effective change management. They underscore the importance of visionary leadership, adaptability, customer focus, cultural transformation, communication, employee engagement, innovation, balance, continuous learning, and data-driven decision making in navigating successful change.

Translating the lessons learned from change pioneers into actionable strategies involves a process of adaptation and application suited to contemporary organizational contexts. This transition from insight to action is vital for leaders seeking to implement effective change management in their organizations. Firstly, developing a clear and inspiring vision based on these lessons is essential. Leaders need to craft a vision that not only aligns with the organization's values and goals but also resonates with and motivates employees. This vision should serve as a compass for all change-related decisions and actions.

Adapting to market changes requires leaders to be consistently observant and responsive. They should cultivate an organizational culture that values agility and quick response to market shifts, ensuring that the company remains competitive and relevant. Emphasizing a customer-centric approach involves regularly gathering and analyzing customer feedback and market data. This information should guide the development and refinement of products, services, and overall business strategies.

Cultural transformation is another crucial strategy. Leaders should work towards creating an environment that supports and rewards adaptability, innovation, and learning. This might involve revising policies, redefining values, and implementing new practices that encourage a change-positive mindset. Effective communication is paramount. Leaders should develop a communication plan that clearly articulates the reasons for change, the benefits it brings, and the steps involved in the process. Regular and transparent communication can help in reducing uncertainty and building trust among stakeholders.

Empowering employees to take an active role in the change process is another key strategy. This can be achieved by involving them in decision-making, encouraging initiative, and providing opportunities for them to contribute their ideas and skills. Innovation should be nurtured as a core organizational value. Leaders should encourage creative thinking and risk-taking, providing the necessary resources and support for experimentation and development of new ideas. Balancing short-term needs with the long-term vision of the organization involves careful planning and prioritization. Leaders should ensure that immediate operational requirements do not overshadow the strategic goals of the change initiative.

Promoting a culture of continuous learning and improvement is essential. This can be done through regular training programs, workshops, and learning opportunities that keep employees up-to-date and aligned with the organization's evolving needs. Lastly, adopting a data-driven approach in decision-making ensures that strategies are grounded in factual insights. Leaders should leverage data analytics to inform their strategies, assess the impact of change initiatives, and make informed adjustments. The stories and lessons of these pioneers serve not only as a source of knowledge but also as a beacon of inspiration for current and aspiring leaders.

- Embodying the Spirit of Visionary Leadership: Change leaders are encouraged to embody the spirit of visionary leadership demonstrated by these pioneers. This involves having a clear, compelling vision, the courage to challenge the status quo, and the ability to inspire and galvanize others towards a shared goal.

- Embracing Adaptability and Resilience: The journeys of change pioneers underscore the importance of being adaptable and resilient in the face of challenges and uncertainties. Leaders are urged to cultivate these qualities, understanding that the path of change is often unpredictable and requires the ability to pivot strategies and persevere through difficulties.

- Fostering a Culture of Innovation and Continuous Learning: Just as change pioneers have fostered cultures of innovation and learning within their organizations, today's leaders are motivated to do the same. Encouraging creativity, experimentation, and learning from both successes and failures are crucial in driving sustainable change.

- Engaging and Empowering Teams: Leaders are inspired to actively engage and empower their teams, as the pioneers have done. Involving employees in the change process, valuing their contributions, and fostering a sense of ownership and collaboration are key to effective change management.

- Leading with Empathy and Integrity: The narratives of successful change leaders often highlight the importance of leading with empathy and integrity. Understanding and addressing the concerns and needs of employees, stakeholders, and customers is vital in building trust and sustaining change.

- Staying Committed to the Long-Term Vision: As demonstrated by the pioneers, maintaining focus on the long-term vision, even when faced with short-term challenges, is essential for successful change leadership. This commitment ensures that the organization stays aligned with its strategic objectives and realizes its envisioned transformation.

As we draw inspiration from the stories of these change pioneers, it becomes evident that the journey of change leadership is both challenging and rewarding. It requires a blend of strategic foresight, operational excellence, and personal attributes like resilience, empathy, and integrity.

Chapter 9: The Future of Change Leadership

In Chapter 9, "The Future of Change Leadership," we embark on a journey to explore the emerging trends in change management that are shaping the way organizations approach transformation in the modern era. This exploration is crucial in preparing leaders and organizations to adapt to the evolving landscape of change.

One of the key trends is the increasing importance of digital transformation. As technology continues to advance at a rapid pace, organizations are finding it essential to integrate new digital solutions into their operations. This encompasses everything from leveraging big data and analytics for informed decision-making to adopting artificial intelligence and machine learning for operational efficiency and innovation. Another significant trend is the growing emphasis on agility and flexibility. The traditional, hierarchical approach to change management is giving way to more agile methodologies that allow for quicker responses to market changes and customer needs. This shift involves adopting practices that enable faster decision-making, iterative development, and a more fluid approach to project management.

Employee engagement and participation in change initiatives are becoming increasingly important. Organizations are recognizing that successful change is not just top-down but requires active involvement from employees at all levels. This approach leads to greater buy-in, more effective implementation of change, and better alignment with organizational goals. Sustainability and social responsibility are also becoming integral to change management. There is a growing expectation for organizations to not only drive financial success but also contribute positively to environmental and social issues. This trend is leading to changes in business models, practices, and corporate cultures that prioritize sustainability and ethical considerations.

The emphasis on mental health and well-being is another emerging trend. Change can be stressful for employees, and there is an increasing recognition of the need to support mental health and well-being during periods of transformation. This includes providing resources, creating supportive environments, and ensuring that change processes do not negatively impact employee well-being. Personalized and continuous learning for employees is gaining traction as a critical component of change management. As roles and skills requirements evolve rapidly, providing ongoing, personalized learning opportunities is essential for keeping the workforce adaptable and skilled.

The role of data in change management is becoming more pronounced. The use of data analytics to guide decision-making, track progress, and measure the impact of change initiatives is proving to be invaluable. Data-driven insights enable organizations to make more informed decisions, anticipate challenges, and tailor change strategies effectively. Chapter 9 delves into the emerging trends in change management, highlighting the critical areas that leaders and organizations must focus on to stay ahead in a rapidly changing world. These trends underscore the need for adaptability, innovation, inclusivity, sustainability, and a data-driven approach in leading successful change initiatives.

These trends reflect the evolving nature of business, technology, and society, offering new perspectives and approaches for effective change leadership.

1. Digital Transformation Acceleration: One of the most significant trends is the rapid acceleration of digital transformation across all sectors. The COVID-19 pandemic has acted as a catalyst, prompting organizations to rapidly adopt digital technologies to adapt to new ways of working, serving customers, and maintaining operations. This trend extends beyond mere technology adoption, encompassing the digitalization of entire business processes and models.

2. Increased Focus on Agile Methodologies: The adoption of agile methodologies is becoming more widespread, moving beyond software development into broader organizational contexts. Agility in change management allows for more flexible planning, iterative development, rapid response to feedback, and quicker adaptation to changing circumstances.

3. Rise of Remote and Hybrid Work Models: Remote and hybrid work models are becoming a permanent feature for many organizations. This shift necessitates changes in how organizations manage teams, maintain productivity, and foster a cohesive company culture in a dispersed work environment.

4. Emphasis on Employee Experience and Engagement: There is a growing understanding that successful change hinges on employee experience and engagement. Organizations are focusing more on understanding and addressing the human side of change, ensuring that employees are supported, heard, and involved in the change process.

5. Sustainability as a Strategic Priority: Sustainability is increasingly being recognized as a critical element of business strategy and change management. Organizations are integrating environmental, social, and governance (ESG) considerations into their business models and operations, responding to both societal expectations and regulatory requirements.

6. Data-Driven Decision Making and Analytics: The use of data analytics in change management is gaining traction. Organizations are leveraging data to gain insights into employee behavior, operational efficiency, and market trends to inform and tailor their change strategies.

7. Personalization of Learning and Development: With the rapid pace of change in skills requirements, there is a trend towards more personalized and continuous learning and development opportunities for employees. This approach helps in building

a more agile and skilled workforce, capable of adapting to new challenges and roles.

8. Focus on Mental Health and Wellbeing: Recognizing the impact of change on mental health and wellbeing, organizations are incorporating strategies to support employee wellness into their change management approaches. This trend reflects a broader shift towards acknowledging and addressing the psychological aspects of organizational change.

These latest trends and developments indicate a dynamic shift in the field of change management, emphasizing the need for agility, digital readiness, sustainability, data-driven strategies, and a focus on the human aspects of change. Understanding and embracing these trends is crucial for contemporary leaders to effectively guide their organizations through the complexities of modern change initiatives. A notable shift is the movement from top-down to more collaborative change models. Traditionally, change initiatives were often dictated by senior leaders, but there's a growing trend towards inclusivity, where inputs from various organizational levels are encouraged and valued. This collaborative approach leads to greater engagement and a more effective implementation of change.

Agility, once a domain specific to software development, is now being applied broadly in organizational change management. This signifies a move away from rigid, long-term planning towards flexible, iterative approaches that allow for swift responses to market changes and customer feedback, facilitating quicker adaptations. Digital transformation has become integral to change management strategies. Organizations are increasingly weaving digital tools and technologies into their change initiatives, whether it's for enhancing internal processes, improving customer experiences, or developing new business models.

There's also a shift in perspective, viewing change not as a discrete project but as a continuous process. This ongoing approach to change management recognizes the constant nature of change in modern business, demanding perpetual readiness for adaptation and evolution. The human aspect of change, particularly the focus on culture and employee well-being, is receiving more attention. Successful change is now seen as a balance between strategy, process, and cultural transformation. This includes understanding the impact of change on employees and ensuring systems are in place to support well-being and resilience.

The use of data analytics in guiding change efforts is becoming more prevalent. Organizations are leveraging data to understand the impact of change initiatives, predict outcomes, and make informed, evidence-based decisions. Sustainability and social responsibility are increasingly being integrated into change management. Organizations are aligning their change efforts with broader environmental and societal goals, recognizing that long-term success is intertwined with sustainable and ethical practices.

These evolving approaches to change reflect a broader shift in how organizations perceive and manage transformation, highlighting the importance of adaptability, inclusivity, and a holistic view of success in the modern business environment. Leaders who embrace and adapt to these changes can more effectively steer their organizations through the complexities and opportunities of today's dynamic world.

In the modern era, technological advancements have had a profound impact on change leadership, significantly altering how change is managed and implemented in organizations. These advancements are not only reshaping operational processes but also influencing the strategic direction and cultural dynamics of businesses. One of the primary impacts is the acceleration of change itself. Technologies such as artificial intelligence, machine learning, and cloud computing have led to rapid innovations and disruptions across industries. Leaders must now navigate an environment where change occurs at an unprecedented pace, requiring quicker decision-making and more agile response strategies. Technological advancements have also democratized information and data, making them more accessible throughout organizational hierarchies. This shift empowers employees at all levels, fostering a more informed and engaged workforce. For change leaders, this means managing a more knowledgeable and, often, expectant team, requiring transparent communication and collaborative decision-making processes.

The rise of digital tools and platforms has transformed communication within organizations. Change leaders now have access to a variety of platforms for real-time communication and collaboration, allowing for more effective coordination and engagement with teams, especially in dispersed or remote work settings. Data analytics and business intelligence tools are playing a crucial role in change management. Leaders can leverage these tools to gain insights into employee behaviors, operational efficiency, and market trends, enabling more informed decision-making. This data-driven approach helps in tailoring change initiatives to be more effective and reduces the risk of unforeseen challenges.

Technology has changed the skill sets required for effective leadership. Today's leaders must not only be proficient in traditional leadership competencies but also be adept at understanding and leveraging technology. This includes staying updated on the latest technological trends and understanding how they can impact business operations and strategies. Technology has expanded the possibilities for personalization and customization in change management. Leaders can now use technology to design personalized training and development programs, ensuring that employees have the skills and knowledge needed to adapt to new systems and processes.

While technology offers numerous tools and capabilities for facilitating change, it also brings challenges. Leaders must address issues such as digital literacy, privacy concerns, cybersecurity risks, and the potential for technology to create disconnects within the workforce. Technological advancements have dramatically changed the landscape of change leadership. They provide powerful tools and capabilities that, if effectively leveraged, can significantly enhance the management and implementation of change. However, they also require leaders to develop new skills and approaches to navigate the digital age effectively. Adapting to these technological changes is essential for leaders aiming to guide their organizations successfully through the complexities of modern-day transformation.

As the business world evolves, so too must the skills and competencies of change leaders. Future-proofing these abilities is essential for navigating the challenges of tomorrow's organizational landscapes. To stay relevant and effective, change leaders must adopt a range of strategies. Developing a continuous learning mindset is crucial. The pace of change in technology and market dynamics requires leaders to be lifelong learners. Staying updated with the latest trends, theories, and practices in change management and related fields is no longer optional but a necessity. Embracing technological proficiency is another key strategy. Change leaders should not only be familiar with the latest technologies but also understand how these can be leveraged for effective change management. This includes everything from data analytics tools to communication platforms and project management software.

Cultivating emotional intelligence remains as important as ever. The ability to understand and manage one's emotions, and to empathize with others, is vital in leading teams through change, especially in times of uncertainty and stress. Strengthening resilience and adaptability is essential in a world where change is the only constant. Leaders must be able to bounce back from setbacks and adapt their strategies in response to new information or changing circumstances. Enhancing collaboration and communication skills is imperative in an increasingly connected world. Leaders should be able to effectively communicate their vision, engage stakeholders at all levels, and foster a collaborative environment conducive to change. Nurturing a culture of innovation within the organization is a forward-thinking approach. Leaders should encourage creative thinking and experimentation, creating a safe space for new ideas and accepting that failure is often part of the innovation process.

Focusing on ethical leadership and corporate responsibility is increasingly important. As societal expectations shift, leaders need to ensure that their strategies and actions are not only effective but also ethically sound and socially responsible. Developing a global perspective is beneficial, especially for organizations operating in or affecting multiple countries. Understanding different cultural contexts and global market dynamics can help leaders make more informed decisions and effectively manage change on a larger scale.

The ability to withstand evolving challenges and adapt to new circumstances is a critical competency in navigating the complexities of modern organizational change. Resilience in change leadership involves the capacity to recover quickly from difficulties and setbacks. It means maintaining a steady course in the face of adversity and being able to bounce back stronger. This resilience is fostered through a mindset that views challenges as opportunities for learning and growth, rather than as insurmountable obstacles. Adaptability, on the other hand, refers to the ability to adjust to new conditions. In the context of change leadership, it means being open to new ideas, willing to alter strategies in response to changing circumstances, and being flexible in approach. Adaptability is crucial in a business landscape where technological advancements and market dynamics can rapidly shift the playing field.

To build resilience, change leaders should focus on developing a strong support network within and outside the organization. This network can provide guidance, support, and perspective during challenging times. Additionally, practicing self-care and stress management techniques is vital for maintaining personal well-being and resilience. Developing a culture of continuous learning within the organization is also key to building resilience and adaptability. Encouraging employees to upskill, reskill, and embrace lifelong learning helps in creating an agile and adaptable workforce capable of handling change. Emphasizing clear and transparent communication is another strategy to foster resilience. Openly discussing the challenges and uncertainties of change helps in building trust and ensures that employees feel supported and valued during the transition process.

Encouraging a culture of experimentation and innovation within the organization can also enhance adaptability. By creating an environment where risk-taking is supported and failures are viewed as learning opportunities, leaders can encourage flexibility and innovative thinking. Adopting a proactive approach to change, where potential risks and opportunities are continually assessed and strategies are adjusted accordingly, can significantly enhance adaptability. Embracing cutting-edge instruments and tools is becoming increasingly important. These advanced tools offer new possibilities for enhancing the efficiency and effectiveness of change initiatives, allowing leaders to navigate the complexities of organizational transformation with greater precision and insight.

Modern change management tools extend beyond traditional project management software. They now include advanced data analytics platforms, artificial intelligence (AI) systems, and collaborative digital workspaces. These tools can provide deeper insights into organizational dynamics, employee engagement, and the impact of change initiatives, enabling more informed decision-making. Data analytics platforms, for example, allow leaders to track and analyze various metrics related to the change process, such as employee performance, engagement levels, and operational efficiency. This data can help in identifying areas of resistance, predicting potential challenges, and measuring the success of change efforts. AI and machine learning tools are being used to predict outcomes of change initiatives and to provide personalized recommendations for leaders. They can analyze vast amounts of data to identify patterns and trends that might not be immediately apparent, offering strategic insights that can guide the direction of change efforts.

Collaborative digital workspaces and communication tools have become essential, especially with the rise of remote and hybrid work models. These platforms facilitate seamless communication and collaboration among team members, regardless of their physical location, ensuring that everyone stays aligned and connected throughout the change process. Virtual and augmented reality technologies are also emerging as powerful tools in change management, particularly for training and development. They provide immersive learning experiences that can be particularly effective for understanding new processes or for simulating different scenarios in a controlled environment.

Cloud-based solutions are enabling more agile and scalable approaches to change management. By leveraging the cloud, organizations can ensure that their change management tools are always accessible and up-to-date and can be easily scaled as the organization grows or as needs change. While these advanced tools offer numerous benefits, leaders must also be mindful of the challenges they present, such as ensuring data privacy and security, managing the learning curve associated with new technologies, and ensuring that the human element of change is not overshadowed by technological solutions.

In embracing these cutting-edge instruments and tools for change management, leaders are equipped to make more data-driven, strategic decisions, enhance collaboration and communication, and provide engaging and effective training experiences. This adoption of advanced technology is pivotal in driving successful change in today's rapidly evolving business landscape. As the business landscape continues to evolve, so do the paradigms and expectations in change leadership. Today's leaders face a myriad of new challenges and opportunities, requiring them to adapt their approaches and strategies to navigate these shifts successfully.

The first significant shift is the move from traditional, hierarchical models of leadership to more collaborative and inclusive styles. Modern change leaders are expected to be facilitators who empower teams, encourage diverse perspectives, and foster a culture of shared ownership in change processes. This shift calls for leaders to be more empathetic, approachable, and open to feedback, breaking down the traditional barriers between different levels of an organization. There is also an increasing emphasis on ethical leadership and social responsibility. Leaders are now expected not only to drive profitability but also to ensure that their organizations positively impact society and the environment. This shift has brought sustainability and ethical considerations to the forefront of business strategies, including change initiatives.

Technological proficiency has become a new standard for change leaders. With the rapid advancement of digital technologies, leaders are expected to be knowledgeable and savvy about the latest tools and trends. This includes understanding how technology can be leveraged to facilitate change processes, enhance communication, and drive efficiency. Change leaders are also navigating a new reality where change is constant and rapid. This dynamic environment demands agility and the ability to pivot strategies quickly in response to new information or changing market conditions. Leaders must foster a culture of resilience and flexibility, enabling their organizations to thrive in the face of continuous change.

The growing complexity of global markets and the increasing diversity within workplaces require leaders to have a broader, more global perspective. Leaders must be cognizant of different cultural contexts and adapt their change management approaches accordingly. This global mindset is essential for organizations operating in, or impacting, multiple countries.

The expectations around transparency have heightened. Stakeholders now demand greater openness and clear communication about the reasons for change, the benefits it brings, and the impact it will have. Leaders must ensure transparency in their decision-making processes and communication strategies to build trust and gain buy-in for change initiatives. There is a shift towards a more holistic view of employee well-being. Leaders are expected to consider the emotional and psychological impact of change on employees and to provide support mechanisms to help them navigate the transition. This approach recognizes that the success of change initiatives is closely tied to the well-being and engagement of the workforce.

Navigating these shifting paradigms and expectations requires leaders to be adaptive, empathetic, technologically adept, ethically minded, globally aware, transparent, and considerate of their employees' well-being. By embracing these evolving aspects of change leadership, leaders can effectively guide their organizations through the complexities and opportunities of the modern business environment.

As we conclude this chapter on the future of change leadership, the focus shifts to thriving in an environment characterized by constant change and evolution. In today's rapidly transforming world, the ability of leaders and organizations to not just adapt to change but to thrive within it is crucial for long-term success and sustainability.

Thriving in this dynamic environment requires a mindset shift. Leaders and organizations must view change not as a disruptive force to be managed, but as an ongoing opportunity for growth and innovation. This perspective fosters a proactive approach to change, where leaders are consistently seeking ways to improve, evolve, and stay ahead of the curve. Building a culture that embraces change is foundational to thriving in this environment. This culture encourages experimentation, values learning from both successes and failures, and views change as an integral part of the organizational journey. Such a culture also supports resilience, helping teams and individuals to bounce back and persist in the face of challenges.

Continuous learning and development are key to thriving in an ever-changing landscape. Leaders must commit to their own ongoing development and foster an environment where employees are encouraged to acquire new skills, stay abreast of industry trends, and continuously evolve their capabilities. This commitment to learning ensures that the organization as a whole remains agile and adaptable. Leveraging technology is also essential in this context. By staying updated with technological advancements and integrating relevant tools and systems, organizations can enhance their efficiency, improve decision-making processes, and maintain a competitive edge.

Prioritizing employee well-being and engagement is another crucial aspect. Change can be stressful, and leaders must ensure that they are supporting their teams through transitions, addressing concerns, and maintaining open lines of communication. A workforce that feels supported and valued is more likely to embrace change and contribute positively. Adopting a data-driven approach in decision-making helps organizations to navigate change more effectively. By relying on data and analytics, leaders can make more informed decisions, anticipate trends, and tailor their strategies to meet evolving needs.

Maintaining flexibility and agility in strategic planning allows organizations to respond swiftly to unexpected changes and seize new opportunities as they arise. This means being willing to revisit and revise strategies, staying open to new ideas, and being ready to pivot when necessary. Thriving in an environment of constant change and evolution involves cultivating a change-positive culture, committing to continuous learning, leveraging technology, prioritizing employee well-being, adopting a data-driven approach, and maintaining strategic flexibility. By embodying these principles, leaders and organizations can not only navigate the complexities of today's business environment but also emerge stronger, more innovative, and more resilient.

Conclusion

As we reach the conclusion of "Leading the Change Revolution: Initiating and Sustaining Transformation," it's a moment to pause and reflect on the journey we've undertaken. This journey through the intricacies of change leadership has traversed various dimensions, from understanding the fundamental nature of change to embracing the latest trends and strategies in change management. Leading change is not merely about managing transitions or implementing new processes; it's about guiding organizations through a journey of transformation. This journey is filled with challenges and opportunities, requiring leaders to continuously adapt, learn, and grow. It's about making decisions that not only affect the immediate future but also pave the way for long-term sustainability and success.

Throughout this exploration, we've delved into the importance of understanding the psychological, cultural, and strategic aspects of change. We've examined how leaders can effectively navigate these elements, employing empathy, communication, and strategic foresight. The role of change leadership extends beyond the boundaries of traditional management; it's about inspiring, motivating, and guiding people towards a shared vision. We've also looked at how the digital age has transformed change leadership, bringing new tools, technologies, and methodologies to the forefront. These advancements offer tremendous opportunities for enhancing the efficiency and impact of change initiatives, but they also come with their own set of challenges and demands.

At the heart of this journey is the recognition that change is an inevitable and constant element of the business landscape. Embracing change, therefore, is not an option but a necessity for leaders who aspire to drive their organizations forward in an ever-evolving world. As we conclude, it's important to acknowledge that the journey of change leadership does not end here. The landscape of change is continuously shifting, and as leaders, the need to stay informed, agile, and responsive is ever-present. The insights and strategies discussed in this book provide a foundation, but the real test of change leadership lies in application, experimentation, and adaptation in the real world.

Leading the change revolution is an ongoing process of learning, growing, and evolving. It's about facing challenges head-on, seizing opportunities, and always striving to be better. As we move forward, let's carry with us the lessons learned, the insights gained, and the inspiration to continue leading change with courage, wisdom, and resilience. As we bring "Leading the Change Revolution: Initiating and Sustaining Transformation" to a close, it's essential to recapitulate the key insights and lessons that have emerged throughout this exploration of change leadership.

1. Embracing Change as a Constant: One of the fundamental insights is recognizing change as an ongoing and inevitable aspect of organizational life. Leaders must not only accept but embrace change as a driving force for growth and innovation.

2. Importance of Visionary Leadership: The role of visionary leadership in driving change cannot be overstated. A clear, compelling vision is crucial for guiding and inspiring teams through the transformation process. Leaders must articulate this vision effectively and rally their teams around it.

3. Psychological Aspects of Change: Understanding the psychological impact of change on individuals and teams is vital. Leaders must acknowledge and address the human emotions and responses that change initiatives can evoke, employing empathy and support throughout the change journey.

4. Fostering a Culture of Adaptability and Learning: Creating a culture that values adaptability, continuous learning, and innovation is key to sustaining change. This involves encouraging an environment where new ideas are welcomed, and failures are viewed as learning opportunities.

5. Strategic Communication and Engagement: Effective communication and stakeholder engagement are pivotal. Transparent, consistent communication and active involvement of stakeholders at all levels ensure buy-in and facilitate smoother transitions.

6. Leveraging Technology and Data: The use of cutting-edge technology and data analytics has become integral in modern change management. These tools enhance the efficiency and effectiveness of change initiatives, enabling data-driven decision-making and streamlined processes.

7. Building Resilience and Agility: Cultivating resilience and agility in the face of change is crucial for both leaders and organizations. This involves being able to quickly adapt to new challenges, bounce back from setbacks, and stay agile in a dynamic business environment.

8. Ethical Leadership and Social Responsibility: The growing emphasis on ethical leadership and social responsibility in change management reflects a broader societal shift. Leaders must ensure that their change initiatives align with ethical standards and contribute positively to society and the environment.

9. Personal and Organizational Growth: Finally, change leadership is an avenue for personal and organizational growth. Leaders must embrace the personal development that comes with leading change and view each initiative as an opportunity to strengthen and evolve the organization.

These insights and lessons form the crux of effective change leadership. They provide a comprehensive framework for leaders who are tasked with navigating the complexities of change in today's fast-paced and ever-evolving business world. As we move forward, these lessons serve as guiding principles, equipping leaders with the knowledge, skills, and mindset needed to lead successful and transformative change initiatives.

Reflection is an integral part of the learning process, providing an opportunity to consolidate the insights gained and to contemplate application in real-world scenarios. Reflecting on personal growth involves examining how one's perspectives and understanding of change leadership have evolved. Readers should consider how their views on the nature of change, the role of a leader in guiding change, and the dynamics of organizational transformation may have shifted or deepened through the course of this book.

It's beneficial to think about the key areas of growth and development. Ask yourself questions like: How has my approach to leading change evolved? What new strategies or concepts have I learned that I can apply to future initiatives? Have I identified areas where I need further development or learning? This introspection can help solidify the learning and identify clear action steps for continuous improvement.

Consider the challenges and opportunities of implementing the lessons learned in your organizational context. Reflect on how you might apply these insights to real-world situations, the potential obstacles you might face, and how you could overcome them. This reflection should also extend to your leadership style and interpersonal skills. Consider how the concepts discussed, such as empathy, communication, and stakeholder engagement, resonate with your personal leadership approach and how you might integrate these into your practice.

Reflecting on personal growth is not just about acknowledging what has been learned but also about recognizing the journey ahead. Change leadership is an ongoing process, with each experience offering new learning opportunities. Embrace the notion that as a change leader, your journey is continuously evolving. Take a moment to acknowledge the progress you have made. Becoming an effective change leader is a journey that requires time, effort, and commitment. Recognizing your growth along this path is important for maintaining motivation and momentum. We encourage readers to view their journey in change leadership as a continuous cycle of learning, application, reflection, and growth. The insights and lessons from this book are steppingstones in this ongoing journey. As you move forward, carry these lessons with you, remain open to new learning, and embrace the challenges and opportunities that come with leading change. It's also essential to underscore the lasting impact of transformational change leadership. The role of a change leader extends far beyond the immediate objectives of specific initiatives; it encompasses shaping the future trajectory of organizations, impacting the lives of employees, and often contributing to broader societal change.

Transformational change leadership is about creating a legacy. It involves implementing changes that not only address current challenges but also pave the way for future growth and innovation. Leaders who approach change with a transformational mindset contribute to building organizations that are resilient, adaptable, and forward-thinking. These organizations are better equipped to navigate the uncertainties of the business world and emerge as industry leaders.

The impact of transformational leadership is also deeply felt at the individual employee level. Leaders who engage, empower, and inspire their teams foster a culture of continuous improvement and personal development. This approach leads to a workforce that is not only more skilled and capable but also more committed and satisfied. Such an environment can elevate the overall performance of the organization and contribute to higher levels of employee retention and satisfaction.

Transformational change leaders often drive innovation that goes beyond the confines of their organizations. By embracing new technologies, exploring new business models, and championing sustainable practices, they contribute to industry-wide shifts and, in some cases, societal progress. The ripple effects of these changes can redefine markets, influence consumer behaviors, and contribute to social and environmental well-being. The leadership style and strategies employed in transformational change also set a precedent for future leaders within the organization. By modeling effective change leadership, current leaders inspire and cultivate the next generation of leaders, ensuring that the legacy of innovation and adaptability continues.

The lasting impact of transformational change leadership cannot be overstated. It is about more than achieving short-term goals; it is about shaping the future of organizations, influencing the lives of individuals, and sometimes, making a mark on the industry and society at large. As change leaders, the opportunity to create such a lasting impact is both a privilege and a responsibility. It requires vision, commitment, and a deep understanding of the transformative power of effective leadership.

The legacy of a change leader is measured not just by the immediate outcomes of their initiatives, but by the enduring positive transformation they instill within their organizations and beyond. This legacy is a testament to their vision, strategy, and the values they embed in the fabric of their teams and processes. Change leaders leave a legacy of positive transformation by creating and nurturing a vision that goes beyond the immediate horizon. This vision often involves transformative goals that align with both organizational objectives and broader societal values, such as sustainability, inclusivity, and innovation. By embedding these values into the organization's culture, change leaders ensure that their vision continues to influence long after specific projects have concluded.

Another key aspect is the development of a resilient and adaptable organizational culture. Change leaders who foster an environment where flexibility, learning, and innovation are part of the everyday ethos build organizations that are better equipped to handle future challenges. This culture becomes their legacy, enabling the organization to continue evolving and succeeding in an ever-changing business landscape. Change leaders also leave a lasting impact through the people they inspire and develop. By mentoring and empowering emerging leaders, they create a pipeline of talent equipped with the skills and mindset to drive future change. This mentorship ensures that the organization continues to benefit from strong leadership and innovative thinking.

The introduction of sustainable and ethical business practices can be a significant part of a change leader's legacy. By prioritizing these practices, leaders not only enhance their organization's reputation and performance but also contribute to positive societal and environmental outcomes. Change leaders who leverage technology and data-driven decision-making set a precedent for future organizational strategies. By integrating these modern approaches into the change management process, they leave a legacy of efficiency, transparency, and informed decision-making.

The legacy of positive transformation is also evident in how change leaders handle challenges and setbacks. Leaders who approach difficulties with resilience, openness to learning, and a commitment to finding solutions inspire a similar approach in their teams and the organization as a whole. Throughout history, there have been numerous instances where visionary change leaders have transformed organizations, leaving indelible marks on their industries and often on society at large. These examples serve as powerful testimonies to the impact of effective change leadership.

One such example is the transformation of Apple Inc. under Steve Jobs. His return to Apple in 1997 marked the beginning of one of the most remarkable corporate turnarounds in history. Under his leadership, Apple shifted its focus to innovation and design, leading to the creation of groundbreaking products like the iPod, iPhone, and iPad. Jobs' emphasis on product quality, customer experience, and brand building transformed Apple into one of the most valuable companies in the world.

Another notable example is the turnaround of Starbucks under Howard Schultz. When Schultz returned as CEO in 2008, Starbucks was struggling with overexpansion and a diluted brand. Schultz revitalized the company by refocusing on customer experience, improving employee training, and expanding the company's international presence. His leadership not only revived Starbucks but also reestablished it as a premier global brand.

Satya Nadella's leadership at Microsoft is a more recent example of transformative change leadership. Since taking over as CEO in 2014, Nadella has shifted Microsoft's focus from a primarily Windows-centric approach to cloud computing and AI technologies. This strategic pivot, combined with a cultural shift towards greater collaboration and openness, has rejuvenated Microsoft, significantly increasing its market value and repositioning it as a leader in the tech industry.

Indra Nooyi, during her tenure as CEO of PepsiCo, led a major strategic and cultural transformation. She shifted the company's focus to healthier products, responding to changing consumer preferences and health trends. Nooyi's vision for a 'Performance with Purpose' approach integrated sustainability into the core business model, balancing short-term profitability with long-term sustainability goals.

These leaders, among others, exemplify the profound impact that visionary change leadership can have on an organization. Their ability to envision a different future, engage and inspire their teams, and execute strategic transformations has not only propelled their companies to new heights but also often reshaped their industries. These examples stand as inspiring models for current and future leaders aiming to embark on transformative change initiatives.

The path of a change leader is both challenging and rewarding, and continuous growth is key to mastering this role. First and foremost, believe in your ability to make a difference. Change leadership is not just about strategies and processes; it's about influencing people and shaping the future. Your vision, determination, and actions have the power to drive meaningful transformation. Stay curious and committed to learning. The landscape of change is ever-evolving, with new challenges and opportunities emerging constantly. Embrace a mindset of lifelong learning, seeking knowledge and insights not just from your field but from a diverse range of sources. This continuous learning will keep you adaptable and innovative.

Build and nurture a strong network of peers and mentors. Change leadership can be a complex journey, and having a support system of individuals who share your challenges and aspirations is invaluable. Engage in communities of practice, attend industry forums, and seek mentorship opportunities. These relationships provide support, inspiration, and a wealth of shared experiences.

Reflect regularly on your experiences. Take time to consider the successes and setbacks you encounter. Reflection is a powerful tool for growth, allowing you to glean insights from your experiences and apply them to future initiatives. Be resilient and maintain a positive outlook. Change initiatives often come with obstacles and resistance. Cultivating resilience will help you navigate these challenges effectively. Stay optimistic and view hurdles as opportunities to learn and improve.

Embrace innovation and be open to new ideas. The most effective change leaders are those who are not afraid to think differently and explore uncharted territories. Encourage creativity and innovation within your team and be willing to take calculated risks. Remember that leading change is as much about personal transformation as it is about organizational transformation. As you guide others through change, take the opportunity to grow as a leader and as a person. Each experience offers lessons that contribute to your development.

In closing, your journey as a change champion is a profound commitment to driving progress and creating a positive impact. With passion, perseverance, and a dedication to continuous growth, you will not only navigate the complexities of change but also emerge as a transformative leader who inspires and leads others towards a brighter future. To maintain engagement and proactivity in leading change, it's crucial to adopt a series of practical strategies woven into your daily leadership practice.

Begin by setting clear and achievable goals for your change initiatives. These should align with both the broader organizational objectives and your vision for change. Tracking progress through defined milestones helps maintain focus and direction. Keeping yourself informed about the latest trends and best practices in your industry and the wider field of change management is essential. This continuous learning not only informs your strategies but also keeps you inspired and open to innovation. Actively seeking and valuing feedback from your team, stakeholders, and customers is pivotal. This input provides critical insights into the perception and impact of your change efforts, allowing you to refine your approach and address concerns as they arise.

Cultivating a collaborative environment within your team is another key aspect. Encourage open discussions and the sharing of ideas. This not only fosters innovative solutions but also ensures that team members feel involved and invested in the change process. Communication is a cornerstone of effective change leadership. Keeping your team and stakeholders informed about developments, challenges, and achievements builds trust and minimizes resistance. Clear and consistent communication is vital in navigating the complexities of change. Being flexible and prepared to adjust your plans in light of new information or unforeseen challenges is crucial. This agility enables you to effectively navigate obstacles and capitalize on emerging opportunities.

Developing your emotional intelligence is equally important. Enhancing skills such as empathy, stress management, and maintaining a positive attitude is vital for leading teams through change and ensuring a healthy work dynamic. Remember that self-care is paramount. Leading change can be demanding, so it's important to look after your physical and mental well-being. This means prioritizing rest, managing stress, and maintaining a balance between work and personal life.

Celebrating successes along the way is also important. Acknowledging and celebrating milestones boosts morale and reinforces the positive aspects of the change journey. Staying committed to your vision for change keeps you and your team motivated, especially when facing challenges. Regularly revisiting and reaffirming the larger purpose behind the change can be a powerful motivator and guide.

Incorporating these approaches into your daily practice as a change leader will help you remain engaged, proactive, and effective in driving and managing change. These strategies enable you not only to handle the intricacies of change but also to inspire and lead others towards successful transformation. The path of change leadership is both demanding and rewarding, filled with challenges that test your resolve and achievements that validate your efforts. Remember, your role as a change leader is pivotal in shaping the future of your organization and, in many ways, the industry and community around you. The decisions you make, the strategies you implement, and the visions you cast have far-reaching effects that go beyond the immediate scope of your projects.

Embrace the journey with all its ups and downs. Each challenge you encounter is an opportunity for growth, and every success, a steppingstone to greater achievements. The landscape of change is ever-evolving, and with it, your skills and perspectives as a leader will continue to develop. Stay committed to your vision and purpose. The road to change is seldom straight, and obstacles are inevitable, but it is your vision and determination that will guide you and your team through. Your passion and commitment can be infectious, inspiring those around you to share in your journey and contribute to the collective goal.

Never underestimate the impact you can have as a change leader. You are not just managing processes; you are influencing lives, shaping cultures, and building legacies. Your leadership can ignite a spark of innovation, drive a movement of transformation, and inspire a generation of future leaders. Continue to learn, adapt, and grow. Change leadership is a continuous learning process, and there is always something new on the horizon. Stay curious, open to new ideas, and willing to adapt your approaches. The best leaders are those who remain students at heart, always eager to grow and improve.

Take a moment to reflect on your journey thus far and the path ahead. Celebrate your progress, learn from your experiences, and look forward to the opportunities and adventures that lie ahead. Your journey as a change leader is unique and valuable, and it is yours to shape and define. Let this book be a catalyst for your continued growth and success in leading change. Carry forward the insights and lessons you have gained, and approach each new challenge with confidence, resilience, and optimism. Your journey as a change leader is a significant one, and you have the potential to make a remarkable impact. Keep moving forward, keep leading change, and keep making a difference.